OPPORTUNITIES

in

Visual Arts
Careers

OPPORTUNITIES

in

AUG   2009

Visual Arts
Careers

REVISED EDITION

MARK SALMON

New York Chicago San Francisco Lisbon London Madrid Mexico City
Milan New Delhi San Juan Seoul Singapore Sydney Toronto

The *McGraw-Hill* Companies

Library of Congress Cataloging-in-Publication Data

Salmon, Mark, 1946-
    Opportunities in visual arts careers / by Mark Salmon. —3rd ed.
        p.   cm.
    Includes bibliographical references.
    ISBN-13: 978-0-07-154529-7 (alk. paper)
    ISBN-10: 0-07-154529-8 (alk. paper)
        1. Art—Vocational guidance—United States.   I. Title.   II. Title: Visual arts
    careers.

    N6505.S34   2008
    702.3'73—dc22   2008024658

1 2 3 4 5 6 7 8 9 10 11 12 13 14 15 16 17 18 19 20   DOC/DOC   0 9 8

ISBN 978-0-07-154529-7
MHID   0-07-154529-8

Interior design by Rattray Design

McGraw-Hill books are available at special quantity discounts to use as premiums
and sales promotions or for use in corporate training programs. To contact a
representative, please visit the Contact Us pages at www.mhprofessional.com.

This book is printed on acid-free paper.

CONTENTS

university programs. Choosing an art school. Getting
into an art college. Scholarships and loans. B.F.A.
degree programs. M.F.A. degree programs. A final
thought.

Acknowledgments

The author wishes to thank the following individuals: Larry Anderson, Marshall Arisman, Linda Bastian, Virginia Beach, William Beckley, Lisa Beers, Stephanie Belcher, Christina Bertoni, Tim Binkley, David Campbell, Corrine Colarusso, Debara Farber, John Farkas, Lilly Filipow, Tom Francis, Pattie Belle Hastings, Allan Hing, Evelyn Hirata, Dolores Howard, Barbara Hutsell, Kay Kallos, Austin Kelly, Tom Klinkowstein, Chip Jameson, Bryan Jefferson, Bob Lobe, Janet Morley, Rene Price, Ned Rifkin, Mark Rokfalusi, Craig Scogen, Laura Seeley, Denise Sfire, Jay Shields, Libby Sims, Stephen Sinon, Jim Spruell, Ying Tan, Jan Taniguchi, Taresa Tantillo, Tommy Thompson, Elizabeth Turk, Shelly Unger, Seranda Vesperman, Norman Wagner, Bucky Wetherell, Elizabeth Wethersby, Jack White, Richard Wilde, and Robert Woertendyke.

In addition, I would like to extend a special note of thanks to Ann Chamberlain and Glenn Gritzer for their valuable help. I also want to take this opportunity to express my warm appreciation to David Rhodes.

INTRODUCTION

IMAGINE THAT YOU have been given an assignment by an art teacher. It asks you to find some free time and to make a list of all of the art you can see in an hour. You go to an art museum and start to make your list. You move through the museum quickly and after an hour have noted some two hundred to three hundred pieces of art—mostly drawings, paintings, and sculpture. Now imagine that you are given another assignment by the same teacher. The basic task is the same, but this time you are asked to find art at a local shopping mall. How much art will you see there?

You notice that several large prints of impressionist paintings have been used to decorate Macy's department store. The bookstore in the mall has some calendars for sale, and each month these calendars feature the work of different artists. And a framing shop sells reproductions of many recognizable art works. But that is about all you discover. After an hour of looking, you cannot find any other works of art. Or can you?

If you expand your conception of what art is and look at the assignment in another light, you will find a great deal that may be regarded as art from an occupational point of view. This will not necessarily fall into the same category as the paintings and drawings at the museum—what you will now see is called *applied art*, and you can find many examples of this kind of work at a mall.

Let's go back to Macy's. First of all, the lettering that gives the word *Macy's* its distinct look was created by an artist who specializes in that kind of design. It serves as the logo or company symbol. Many logos involve lettering, but they don't have to. Most of the stores in the mall have logos that have been designed by a graphic designer. In fact virtually all large corporations have a logo that represents the company or its products. Consider such corporations as McDonald's, Dell Computers, and Verizon, each of which has a logo that helps to identify the company and fix it in the minds of consumers.

But let's get back to Macy's and the mall. Nearly everything that is related to the basic merchandising function of stores depends on such applied arts as graphic design, illustration, and photography. All of the packages for the products that you see in stores, whether they contain perfume, tennis balls, or candles, are created by package designers. The clothing that Macy's and other stores sell is created by fashion designers. Household products of all kinds are created by industrial designers. The layout of the store itself, including the furnishings, the surface coverings on the walls and floors, the display areas and counters, and even the lighting have all been planned by an interior designer.

If you once again shift your attention to the bookstore in the mall, you will find that everything from book covers to the way in which the chapters and pages are set up are the work of designers. Book designers use photographs and illustrations to represent the ideas or events that the publication hopes to convey. Similarly magazines need photographers, illustrators, typographers, and graphic designers to create the images used in articles and stories. Magazines are also heavily dependent on designers who specialize in laying out the format of the pages. All of the advertisements that you see in magazines have also been designed. Each time a new magazine debuts, a designer will be hired to create an original look for the new publication. When you open a copy of *Vanity Fair* or *Newsweek*, think about how much of what you see has been produced by artists.

These various logos, products, packages, clothing, books, magazines, photographs, and interior spaces are all very much a part of the world of commercial or applied art. They are also very much a part of the world in which we live. This notion will change the way you look at your surroundings and also the way you look at art. From this point of view, art is not simply something that is restricted to art museums and galleries. It is something that is basic to the experience of everyday life.

The next time you have cereal, toast, and juice for breakfast, look at the cereal box, the wrapping around the bread, and the carton of juice. All three were designed by commercial artists. In fact when you go to the grocery store, nearly every surface you see—from labels on cans and bottles to the display advertising for products to the physical layout of the store itself—is the product of an applied artist. If you were to take away surface designs and images, including lettering, much of your world would appear to you as an opaque shell. Once you have developed this kind of awareness, you will realize just how often art touches your life each and every day. You will also realize how dependent our culture is on the visual information produced by artists.

However if you now begin to think of applied art as being essentially the same as fine art, you have missed the point. This is not meant to suggest that a painting by Rembrandt and the label on a jar of peanut butter are equivalent, because clearly they are not. Rather we can think of both as occupational areas that have much in common despite their differences. It is also true, however, that there are famous applied artists whose work is greatly respected in the art world and is represented in collections of some of the most important art museums in the world.

All of the work described above was produced by men and women who make livings as applied artists. Applied art, which includes design, has become one of the fastest growing and most important segments of our economy. One reason for this is that good design has itself become a commodity that adds value to the things we buy. In addition, there has been a growing appreciation for the fine arts with more and more art galleries opening up around the country. It is not surprising that the number of people entering the field of art and design is increasing. It is not easy to make a living in art and design, but for individuals with talent and determination, the rewards are worth the effort.

1

ART, CULTURE, AND THE ECONOMY

WHAT DO WE mean when we use the term *visual arts*? The most obvious answer is that visual arts refers to those art forms that are primarily visual in nature, such as painting, photography, sculpture, printmaking, and filmmaking. All of these are considered fine arts. In its current usage, the term *visual arts* also refers to crafts, which are sometimes called *practical arts*. These may include works composed of ceramics and glass, wood, stone, metal, paper, or any of a number of materials. In a broad sense, the term may also include the applied arts of industrial design, graphic design, fashion design, interior design, decorative art, and functional art.

In light of this inclusive definition, we may even say that the visual arts play an important role in the economy, perhaps more so now than at any other time in history. This is because they encompass nearly every aspect of design, marketing, and sales in most aspects of culture.

In order to better understand the close links between art, culture, and the economy, it helps to distinguish two components of culture. While culture includes ideas and values that either are understood on a cognitive level or are felt on an emotional level, those cultural elements are expressed and represented in physical form. For instance, a high school mascot exemplifies how thoughts and feelings about an educational institution may be embodied in an illustration or an object such as a stuffed animal. Consequently, visual representations may have symbolic meaning because they remind people of thoughts and feelings. This is true not only for things like high school mascots but for all other representations of culture as well.

Examples of such representational or symbolic relationships are all around us. Fine art represents an artist's thoughts and feelings, religious symbols stand for powerful ideas and emotions about various forms of god and morality, a nation's flag represents a country and its people, and a corporate logo helps represent a company and its products or services. There are many other examples, and they all share one common characteristic: physical objects have cultural meaning.

This does not mean that objects are always designed to convey meaning. Sometimes meaning is secondary to the intended use of an object, but often it is central to the object itself. Consider clothing as an example. Is the design of clothing mostly about practical issues such as warmth and durability, or is it about making people look and feel good and helping them express their identity? Most of us would agree that both factors are important components in clothing design.

The same may be said about many other consumer products that have practical value but are also representational. Many of the items we choose to decorate our homes serve both practical and personal functions. You may need to buy a window shade to block the bright morning light in the kitchen, but you also want the selection to express your taste and to fit the overall decor of your home. Objects don't always convey the meaning that people intend them to convey—it is possible for an intended meaning to be perceived in a variety of ways. However, the basic point remains true: the representations of culture are infused with meaning.

The term *conspicuous consumption* was coined by the American economist and sociologist Thorstein Veblen, who argued that people acquire commodities in order to display their social standing. While this is undoubtedly true in many cases, people may also select items to convey the impression that they are informed and cultivated, thereby making art into a form of enlightened consumption. Consumer choices in products may help people convey the impression to themselves and to others that they make discerning decisions. Art and design have psychological value because they help people to express or represent things about themselves that imply taste, knowledge, and experience.

Despite the many variables related to art, culture, and the economy, the fact remains that the visual arts are an important part of the economy, not simply because they express our culture but also because they offer so many career opportunities for creative people. In the following chapters you will read about different career options in this exciting field.

What Is Art?

Before you begin to pursue a specific career, you need to learn some things about the field you are planning to enter. Some professions are fairly self-explanatory—most of us can say with some confidence that we understand the basic work of teachers, doctors, and pharmacists. We have all had direct contact with these professionals, and we know at least the basic functions of their work.

But how many of us have had contact with artists? Who are they? What kind of work do they do? How do they make a living? How do they start a career? This book will help you to answer these questions and see if a career in art may be right for you.

Perhaps we should start with a very basic question: what is art? This question yields a variety of answers. The simplest and most direct answer may be one that comes from sociologists, who would say that art is whatever people and social institutions define as being art. If an art gallery, art museum, art college, or art critic calls something "art," and if enough people in society accept this judgment, then by that definition, it is art. Despite its apparent simplicity, however, this definition doesn't take the easy way out. Rather it acknowledges a basic fact that is central to understanding art as a career: art is deeply embedded in the social institutions and cultural life of a society. Understanding this viewpoint will help you to get a good grasp on the economic and occupational issues related to art as a career.

You will find that art as an occupation is deeply connected to galleries, museums, private collections, art colleges, art programs in universities, art critics and magazines, corporate art collections, funding agencies, design companies, advertising and marketing, book and magazine publications, and a host of other social and cultural institutions. Although art is often discussed in highly abstract and conceptual terms, when considering it as a career, it is a good idea to take a very practical approach to the social networks and institutional contexts in which art is embedded.

Expression and Profession

There are other practical conceptions of art, and we will focus on two additional theories that help establish the focus of this book. First, art has traditionally been viewed as a means to express the aesthetic ideas and feelings of the individual. In this respect art is defined as a means of aesthetic self-expression for uniquely gifted individuals. This is especially true of the art that has been produced during the last five hundred years, which has been judged as the unique personal expression of each particular artist. The uniqueness and individuality of the artistic genius has been thought to be of primary importance for creative individuals. When we think of the great artists of the past, such as da Vinci, Vermeer, or Pollack, we are struck by how clearly we can identify their particular works. It has their individual creative stamp, and we know it immediately by sight.

This uniqueness is especially characteristic of fine art works that involve drawing, painting, printmaking, and sculpture, as well as certain kinds of photography and works produced by electronic media. Works of fine art are often individual works of beauty. Although some contemporary artists may consider the idea of art as beauty to be naïve, irrelevant, or dated, it is still a useful way to characterize a large range of fine art works that you might have already seen in books, museums, or galleries.

Contemporary fine artists are often more concerned with representing a wide range of abstract ideas and/or social ideals than they are in producing works of beauty. This approach to art began in the nineteenth century with the development of opposing views of art as an expression of aesthetic ideals versus art as social commentary and criticism.

The concern with aesthetic self-expression may lead artists to a rather conflicted role. On the one hand, artists who want to earn a living through their work must be sensitive to the values and tastes of the public. On the other hand, they attempt to pursue a very personal artistic vision that, for a variety of reasons, may sometimes be at odds with social standards.

This may lead to tension between artistic expression and public acceptance of art, which is especially true in a democratic society where individual freedom creates the possibility of many artistic points of view. As artists engage the values and issues of their time, they may produce work that is controversial, inflammatory, or contrary to social standards. Thus, artists may receive less support for their work from critics, patrons, and agencies than those whose work falls within a broad range of what is typically regarded as acceptable. Issues over the public funding of controversial art testify to this occasional tension between personal aesthetics and public values.

Striking a balance between personal artistic vision and broader public taste can be a significant occupational issue for artists. An artist who chooses to produce work that no one wants to buy may be personally satisfied but have a difficult time sharing that satisfaction with the public. Most people who pursue art as a career are sensitive to public taste and the marketability of their work.

The second basic definition of art focuses less on creative expression and more on the usefulness of art. Since the earliest days of human history, art has had a practical role in serving the needs of people in society. Consider the cave drawings of animals done by early humans. Some art historians think that these drawings were part of a magical ritual that would help people to tame animal spirits, thereby making their prey easier to hunt.

So to get a full picture of the history of art, we need to remember that art has often been used for a variety of practical purposes. It has been used to express ideas, convey information, and design products that people use on a daily basis. Aesthetic concerns are still present in these works, but they are merged with and sometimes subordinate to a variety of functional considerations.

Some eight or nine hundred years ago during the Middle Ages, art was considered to be a practical occupation. It was not thought of in terms of unique creative genius but rather as a craft very much like others, such as weaving, carpentry, or shoemaking. Artists of that period were regarded simply as manual laborers and would typically work as building designers, sign painters, or book illustrators.

Such practical considerations continue to be an important part of the craft tradition of art. Today art that has a practical purpose is sometimes referred to as commercial art, but artists who produce this kind of work usually prefer the term *applied art*. Because certain kinds of applied art such as fashion design or graphic design are intended to be useful, they have not had the same history of antagonism with public taste as some fine art. This doesn't mean that the taste of the consuming public has not exerted pressure on applied artists. The public has often expressed a clear preference for particular design characteristics of the applied arts just as it has with fine art. The fundamental difference, however, is that applied artists belong to an occupational tradition that responds to and tries to satisfy public taste, whereas fine artists belong to an occupational tradition that may be indifferent or even antagonistic to public taste. These differences in attitudes toward public opinion are part of a larger set of issues that have made an impact on the economics of art.

Creative Link

Using the two traditions outlined above as a guide, the world of art can essentially be categorized as fine art or applied art. Fine art includes the kinds of paintings, drawings, or sculpture that you might see in an art museum or gallery. It is what most people think of first when they think of art, and it is evaluated in terms of criteria related to personal creativity and aesthetics as well as visual and thematic relevance. Because contemporary art is sometimes intended as political critique or social commentary, it has increasingly taken on a practical role related to social transformation. There have been similar practical uses of fine art that have made some artists and critics uncomfortable, such as the official art of the former Soviet Union and its use as propaganda. It remains true, however, that most fine art is still guided by aesthetic standards that generally avoid practical considerations.

Applied art involves a wide range of work that is largely but not exclusively concerned with design. The applied arts include such fields as illustration, advertising design, graphic design, fashion design, interior design, art education, and art therapy. Although aesthetic issues are still considered to be very important and have actually been the motivating force behind some important design movements, they are usually seen as enhancing rather than defining the underlying practical value of the applied arts.

That added value is important and should not be taken for granted, because good design does more than simply add an aesthetic dimension to our everyday world. It can also make that world an easier, safer, and more satisfying place in which to live, work, and play. In addition, good design can influence our ability to recognize culturally and economically significant objects and ideas, adding value to our everyday world.

Thus the fine and applied arts share much in common, and aesthetics are important to both. As we have seen, fine art is defined by aesthetic issues. Forms of personal expression are usually only defined as art when they satisfy some basic aesthetic criterion such as beauty or social truth.

But aesthetics are also important to the applied arts because, while they produce a useful product, they are created with a strong sense of good design. The aesthetic impulse of designers and the useful function of what they produce actually complement one another, because good design has become as important to a product's marketability as its functional values. People are no longer content to limit their aesthetic experiences to what they see at an art museum. They now want to surround themselves with good design and to make aesthetic experiences a part of their everyday lives. Automotive companies and clothing manufacturers have known this for a long time, and today the producers of nearly all consumer products understand it as well.

Because the fine and applied arts are informed by aesthetics, they are both the creative extensions of the individual artist or designer. Creativity grows out of an individual impulse that all artists and designers experience intensely and enjoy deeply. If you are currently involved in drawing, painting, photography, or any form of art, you very well may have experienced this creative impulse. The satisfaction that comes from being creative and from living the creative life is an important part of what makes art so fulfilling from an occupational point of view.

Another significant link between fine and applied artists is that both are trained in art colleges or in university art programs and share a similar or overlapping curriculum. In fact students who major in painting, sculpture, graphic design, and illustration will typically have a common first-year curriculum. Fine and applied art students often take classes together, an exposure that can be valuable to both of them.

One reason for this overlap in curriculum is the common issues that both fine and applied artists must address in their work. For example all artists face basic aesthetic problems related to line, color, composition, scale, content, concept development, and creative vision, as well as artistic concerns related to materials and techniques. These elements form the basic visual vocabulary and technical foundation of art, whether it is advertising design, illustration, or sculpture.

Another important link between fine and applied art is that they both reflect the experiences of artists who live and work in a particular cultural period. Artists who belong to the same historical period are exposed to similar cultural experiences that shape their consciousness and artistic vision, resulting in the development of a particular style or period in art. The impact of culture on individual experience lends common themes and elements to artistic works within a style or period. This suggests an interesting role for the artist, who is able to translate the common human experiences into images that others can appreciate on an aesthetic level. In this way artists are able to bridge the gap between the external reality of the everyday world and the subjective aesthetic experience of artistic contemplation.

From an occupational point of view, the nature, structure, and conditions of the work of fine and applied artists also share some characteristics. This is especially true for applied artists who do freelance work. Like fine artists they are self-employed, a fact that dictates the way they conduct their professional lives. In addition artists sometimes begin with a focus on one kind of art and shift to another kind of art later on. Moreover each kind of artist may be influenced by, borrow from, or be interrelated with the other. In fact, there are a variety of important connections and elements in common between fine art and commercial art. The point, however, is not to argue the ways in which fine and applied art are alike or different but rather to make the general point that the term *art* is broad enough to include them both.

2

CREATIVITY AND CAREERS

ONE OF THE first steps in understanding the occupational aspects of art as a career is to consider how art is produced, a process that can be as individual as each artist. There is more to understanding how art is made than learning how an artist thinks, feels, and acts during the creative process. There are other elements that contribute to the artistic process and its development that should also be considered.

The artistic process may vary tremendously depending on the particular artist, which is what we might expect of such a highly individualistic endeavor. Some artists work at night while others prefer to work during the day. Some need music for inspiration, and others require the reassuring calm of silence. Some artists get their ideas directly from life, and others rely on their imaginations.

Despite their differences, most successful artists share some common elements in the creative process. The key word here is *successful*. As in other fields, success in art is the result of hard work as much as it is the result of talent. Not everyone who attempts a career in art is successful, but it is important to remember that success should not be measured solely in terms of career issues. It also may be measured by such factors as personal growth and self-discovery. While the information in the following sections doesn't provide a formula for a great career in art or design, it includes some important points that should be considered carefully.

A Commitment to Art

Some of the elements that contribute to success in art are hard to measure. Foremost among these is commitment. If you make a commitment to art, you must have the motivation to work hard toward shaping your future. The primary element of this commitment is the love of art. It doesn't make sense to consider pursuing an artistic career unless you really love to produce art—the joy of art and the art-making process are important aspects of the psychological rewards of the profession.

As you consider a possible career, ask yourself this simple question: "How important is it for me to make art, and how often do I make it?" If you love art but don't really like to produce it, then perhaps you might prefer working as an art historian, art critic, art dealer, or art teacher. If you do make art but don't really enjoy doing it, you should carefully consider your motivation. You may be going through the motions to make someone else happy or still be following a path that you once thought you wanted to pursue. In either case you will probably find it very difficult to develop the genuine commitment you need to become a successful artist.

Commitment to art is sustained not only by the love of art but also by the various rewards that involvement in art can provide.

These rewards may be both intrinsic (the satisfaction of making art) and extrinsic (the professional rewards that come with career success). The goal of this book is to help you understand the many career opportunities in the visual arts that make it personally as well as professionally rewarding.

A commitment to art really means the willingness to pursue long-range goals. A shared characteristic of some of the professions is a lengthy training period. Training in art may begin unofficially at an early age. For example you may have enjoyed playing with crayons or paints as a child, or you might have become involved with art in high school. Whenever you started, you recognized that you love art and now must be willing to stay with it.

Unlike the world of music, in which very young children may become prodigies, there are very few examples of successful artists who did not have extensive training and a great deal of experience. Therefore it is important to acknowledge that it may take a considerable length of time before you become accomplished enough to make your art career pay off. Some are fortunate enough to begin to develop successful careers during or right after attending art school; for others, it takes a combination of time, hard work, and some aggressive entrepreneurial know-how.

Importance of Hard Work

Perhaps the single most important factor that contributes to success in the field of art and design is hard work. While this might seem obvious, unfortunately it is sometimes obscured by naïve images of the artist living an unstructured life, ignoring any responsibilities except those demanded by the work. Artists have sometimes been perceived as spontaneous and undisciplined, and our culture has long associated creativity with play. We sometimes speak, for example, of playing with a new idea.

Thinking of art as the product of undisciplined or playful bohemians is a stereotype that was perhaps created by people who saw the artist's job as much easier than their own daily grind, because spending the workday with paints, charcoals, or clay seemed much more like fun than labor. The image may have been reinforced by films about the near-obsessive working methods of Vincent Van Gogh or Jackson Pollack, to name two artists who seemed to care only about their craft at the expense of all else.

As romantic as these stereotypes may be, they are far from the norm. Creating art does require long hours and hard work, including sustained concentration and a fully conscious involvement in the activity. But artists who hope to support themselves through their work must also pay attention to the real world, which includes maintaining personal and professional relationships and paying bills.

At the end of the day, artists and designers often feel both deeply satisfied and very tired. If you want to pursue art as a career, you must be prepared to work long and hard to achieve your professional objectives. If you are thinking about applying to an art college or to a university art program, you need to understand what lies ahead and begin to develop good work habits right now, not only in art but in all of your academic subjects. The application procedure to art colleges and art programs in universities will be discussed in detail in subsequent chapters of this book.

Need for Self-Discipline

If you were to get a job with a design company, you would have to work according to your employer's schedule and finish specified assignments within a set period of time. Although this might not fit into the artistic life that you may imagine, in many ways this type of work environment is more comfortable than you may realize. One reason is because working for a company involves an organizational structure and culture much like what you've probably already experienced at school.

However you feel about school, you may recognize that it is a familiar, stable, and relatively predictable environment. In short, you know what you need to do and when you need to do it, so it is understandable that a similar work environment might be comfortable. Not only are these settings relatively stable and predictable, they also provide a steady paycheck—good work habits are reinforced by the requirements and rewards of the job. As in school, your work environment will be relatively safe and secure.

For fine artists and freelance designers, however, the situation is quite different. Such workers don't have a supervisor determining their daily activities, which may sound very attractive. If you didn't like meeting deadlines for term papers and other assignments, then you may like the idea of not having a boss giving you creative assignments. While it is true that some people perform best working on their own, this is not quite as easy as it sounds. If you don't have a supervisor, you must be able to rely on yourself to set assignments and make sure they are completed on time. You must also be responsible for quality control, because no one will be standing over your shoulder telling you to try harder or do better. If you are a designer or an artist selling your own work, you will also be responsible for getting your own clients.

Perhaps the best way to sum up what is required by being on your own is that you must demand as much of yourself, if not more, than other people would demand of you. No one else will hold you accountable. In short, if you are on your own and want to be successful, you must learn to be self-disciplined and self-reliant.

Consider Your Talent

Perhaps by now you can guess why talent is not mentioned as the primary factor that determines success for an artist or designer. The world is full of talented people. Many may have had promising futures but never became artists because they were not truly committed to art, did not work hard enough, or lacked self-discipline. As in any professional field, success in art is driven by hard work and determination, perhaps more so than by any other factor. Before you consider the role of talent in an art career, you must understand that talent by itself is never enough to take you beyond the first few steps in achieving your goals.

It remains true that different people have different levels of artistic ability, and more talented people generally do better than those with less talent. The question you may be asking yourself is, "Do I have enough talent to have a successful career in art or design?" Fortunately you can get some fairly reliable help in answering that question. If you have done some artwork already, you should show it to people who are in a position to give you an informed and unbiased assessment of your ability. These should not necessarily be people in your immediate family or your close friends, who may not always give you the honest opinions you need. It is a better idea to ask an art teacher to look at your work and discuss it with you. You might consult a private art teacher, a high school art teacher, or someone who teaches art in a local college or university. Because assessments of art can vary so much, it is a good idea to consult more than one person. You also need to balance what they say against your own self-assessment and your own commitment to art.

Need for Creative Intelligence

It is commonly believed that there are two sides to art, which is reflected in the fact that we often experience art on an emotional level but discuss it on an intellectual level. Because our emotional responses to art are so direct and immediate, we might assume that the creation of art is fundamentally an emotional experience. While this is true for many artists, it is important to remember that creative intelligence is also part of the process.

Intelligence exists in many forms. It is not exclusively related to the abstract reasoning that we associate with the study of mathematics or philosophy but can also manifest itself in a full range of aesthetic capacities. Artists solve spatial problems, which sometimes involve manipulating an enormously complex set of two- and three-dimensional visual elements. Art production requires a powerful mind that is capable of assessing the complexity of spatial terms.

So artists must anticipate the quality of visual relationships before they are set down on paper, canvas, film, or stone. The problems of artistic synthesis are increased when the challenge of coordinating color, tone, and intensity is added to that of configuring spatial relationships. The artist's mental ability is stretched yet again when formal issues such as line, form, mass, scale, depth, and color are used as the vehicles for expressing ideas through art. It is only through the disciplined application of creative intelligence that talent may be harnessed to produce good art.

Sources of Ideas and Inspiration

Artists and designers do not produce work in a vacuum. They live and work in a world that is a constant source of ideas and inspiration. Artists are particularly observant and therefore may often see things that others do not, finding patterns, textures, structures, objects, and colors that are visually interesting everywhere they look. Artists and designers may see beauty in the patterns of shadows or a collection of toys on a front lawn. The important point is that aesthetic meaning is not an inherent quality of the shadows or toys—it lies in the artist's perception, which is an important part of artistic creativity.

Artistic productivity is not necessarily the automatic result of creative potential, however. It comes about because artists are able to focus that potential on a particular project. Simply put, artists *have* to draw, paint, sculpt, or photograph something, but what should that something be and in what manner should it be created? To answer this question, artists and designers need ideas, which they often find by paying close attention to the world around them.

An artist's personal experiences are an important source of ideas. Works can be inspired by family background, personal ties, social circumstances, economic conditions, religious beliefs, emotional experiences, and political ideals. Sometimes artists are inspired by the effort to reconcile and express the relationship between their inner life and the reality of external conditions, which can make art such an intensely personal experience.

The work of past and present artists is another source of ideas, since artists spend a lot of time looking at the cultural icons of the past. Earlier artists may have addressed ideas that are similar to the concerns of contemporary artists and may, therefore, serve as a valuable reference or source of inspiration. For this reason art history may play an important role as either a guide or point of departure for artistic expression.

Artists also are likely to be knowledgeable about the contemporary art scene for the same kind of reason. In fact, sociologist

Lawrence Shornack once described art production as a process in which artists sometimes work with the imaginary presence of particular artists looking over their shoulders with critical eyes.

Language and Concept Visualization

In the sixteenth and seventeenth centuries, the education of artists changed in a way that impacted the future of art. The training of artists in academies began to emphasize the acquisition of knowledge, including a familiarity with poetry, music, philosophy, history, and mathematics. This had far-reaching consequences, which we will consider more fully when we look at art education. At this point, it is enough to understand the role of learning as a source of artistic ideas.

The written word can bring images to life because language can activate the mind and is the medium through which concepts and concrete reality are visualized. The form of Japanese poetry called haiku is an excellent example of the relationship between language and visual imagery. These short, three-line poems have the power to evoke not only mental pictures but also feelings and ideas. Here is an example of a seventeenth-century haiku by the poet Basho:

> On a leafless bough
> In the gathering autumn dusk:
> A solitary crow!

Just as words may be used to represent visual images, so too can visual images be used to represent the ideas that words convey, because images and ideas can stand for one another. This has critical implications in understanding the role of education in the careers of both fine and applied artists. It means that learning can be one of the most important sources of artistic ideas, so part of your training should include reading as much as possible to develop a rich and lively artistic imagination.

In many ways, the relationship between images and ideas is the foundation for both fine and applied art. One of the important characteristics of fine art is its power to convey feelings or ideas that elevate or illuminate the human condition, which is why symbolism and the interpretation of art are considered to be so important. The applied arts, especially illustration, advertising design, and graphic design, are evaluated on a similar basis. The difference between the two kinds of art, however, is telling. The thoughts and feelings that fine art may evoke are often regarded as its ultimate objective. For the applied arts, by contrast, the ultimate objective is to elicit thoughts and feelings as a way to motivate particular kinds of behavior—especially consumer behavior.

Developing an Idea

The sociologist Howard Becker once made an interesting distinction between art and craft. He argued that art is intended to produce unique or one-of-a-kind pieces of work, while craft has traditionally involved the development of virtuoso skills that enable the craftsperson to make essentially the same thing over and over again in the same way—like making a matched set of bowls or candle holders, for example. Printmaking and photography are also fields in which multiple originals may be produced. In this sense we might say these are fields where art and craft merge.

The idea that fine art always produces unique pieces of work is a bit misleading, however. Although it is true that the particular works of an artist may be unique as pieces of art, they may also be variations on a theme. Such an approach to art or design is sometimes referred to by artists as "developing" or "pushing" an idea. In the previous section, we saw that art and design are produced as a consequence of the aesthetic or artistic expression of an idea. But a single artistic expression does not exhaust all of the possibilities for the ways an idea may be presented. Artists often try as many variations of an artistic idea as they can, especially if their idea sells.

Some artists seem to have a single artistic idea that is so commercially successful they do not seem to change it in any significant way at all. You have probably seen the stick-figures on T-shirts and in advertising that have made artist Keith Haring so well known, or Robert Indiana's iconic LOVE sculptures that have even been used on postage stamps. Sometimes the works are self-conscious efforts to develop the full range of possibilities for an artistic idea and are typically presented as a group of pieces called a *series*.

There is an important point here for those who hope to become artists. Doing a single drawing or painting does not mean that you have learned all that you can from the piece. If you have done something that you like or that you think is interesting, try as many variations of it as you can until you have exhausted all the artistic possibilities you can find. Once you have explored an aesthetic idea fully, move on to new challenges so that your artistic ideas continue to grow and develop.

Evolving and Experimenting

One valuable consequence of developing an idea is that it enables you to move on to other ideas in a series of evolving stages. This happens as you begin to explore an artistic idea, develop the various possibilities that it has to offer, and then experiment with other ideas, building on what has come before. The work that artists produce in this way is more than the expression of artistic development; it also becomes a record of the evolution of their creative lives. Some artists radically change their style and subject matter in a relatively abrupt way. For example, after visiting the rugged Scottish coast, the American artist Winslow Homer switched from painting idyllic rural scenes to the seascapes for which he is best known. But the work of most artists moves progressively forward, with each step along the way a developmental consequence of the struggle to express ideas, explore them fully, and move on to new ideas.

The evolution of an artist's work may also be related to experimentation with technique and materials. Here the challenges posed by an artist's medium may push the work in new directions. The desire for new artistic potential is one reason that artists work in mixed media, because it allows interdisciplinary approaches to art production that often produce creative results.

Craftsmanship of Art

One part of the art-making process that sometimes receives less attention than it should is the craft of art. This refers to the methods and materials of production, including the technical aspects that require practice and skill. There is an important hands-on quality to artistic production that many artists enjoy and acknowledge as essential to the art-making process. Aesthetic theory is interesting and valuable, but it can lose its significance if the artist cannot adequately manipulate the medium.

Each medium has a physical quality that is a source of satisfaction for the artist. Successful painters, sculptors, photographers, printmakers, illustrators, and graphic designers have all mastered the tools and materials of their trade. Even drawing, perhaps especially drawing, has a directness and immediacy in the physical contact of pencil on paper that artists appreciate. Artists must be adept at using their tools and materials if they are to adequately bridge the gap between their artistic vision and what they put on paper.

Computers in Art

Technology has impacted the world of art much as it has so many other professions. Artists may use computers to produce two- and three-dimensional abstract and figurative works by drawing and painting with electronic lines, colors, and shapes. In addition software packages allow the artist to give the surface of rendered objects not only a seemingly limitless array of colors but also a huge variety of textures, degrees of luster or shine, and various levels of brightness. It also can cast a shadow on the surface of an electronically rendered object that has been illuminated by an imaginary light source, which is especially important when an artist is simulating real objects.

Artwork produced by computers may have the same basic appearance as art produced in more traditional ways. An exhibit of computer-generated fine art produced with computers may include a number of pieces that reveal an artistic imagination shaped by earlier use of conventional media. This is true for both abstract and figurative work. In addition computer art is used in mixed media pieces.

Like any art technology, the use of computers may be both liberating and confining for artists. Computer art sometimes has a distinctive look that makes it notably different from conventional art.

It also lacks the actual textured surface qualities that make painting and sculpture so satisfying, and it may not provide the physical pleasure that some artists get from the craft of making art. Although computers can be intriguing and exciting, they remain only one among many of the artists' tools and methods.

A Final Thought

You now know the elements that will be a necessary part of building your career in the visual arts. You must have a strong commitment to art, and you must be willing to commit also to the hard work and self-discipline that are part of any successful venture. Your talent and creativity will serve you well if you are able to combine them with the personal strength needed to pursue the necessary training to work toward gaining experience as an artist. Finally you must be willing to experiment and perhaps change direction along the way as you explore the path that will become your career.

3

Art as a Profession

In the previous two chapters you learned how even the most basic distinctions about art show the various ways in which it may be practiced as a career, and you have seen the creative process from which the arts emerge. But in many instances art is thought of more as a product, as something to enjoy, think about, and discuss. Although we regularly see the end result of art and design in museums, galleries, department and home furnishing stores, magazines, and on television, we may not think of it in occupational terms and consider how people actually make a living as artists.

The issue of earning a living through art is serious, so it is important to understand that art is a professional activity that offers the possibility of many different careers. While it is true that artists may struggle economically, especially in the early years of a career, it is also true that an increasing number of people make a comfortable living as artists. In the remainder of this book, we will explore the ways in which this is accomplished, keeping in mind that a career in art may provide more than financial rewards.

The idea that art can be rewarding beyond providing an income is more important than you might think. Aside from economic considerations, the career that you choose will have psychological factors that directly impact how you experience the work you do. Simply put, we are talking about job satisfaction, which will contribute a great deal to the overall quality of your life. Considering the fact that most people work until at least their early sixties and a growing number work well beyond that, you don't want to spend many years doing something that you don't enjoy. Ideally you will earn a living doing something that is economically rewarding and personally enjoyable.

What Makes Art a Profession?

Before we look at the various career areas in art, we should begin by understanding what kind of work art is. There are useful employment classifications that can tell a lot about the nature of different kinds of work. Consider such categories as blue-collar, clerical, and managerial occupations, each of which has characteristics that tell us something about the fundamental and defining nature of the area of work. Where does art fit into these classifications? And in what ways can it be considered a profession?

A profession is a category of work with basic characteristics that make it distinct from other ways of earning a living. These characteristics define the nature of the work and may include such factors as the length of training required; the theoretical as well as practical nature of that training; the development of it as a career, which increases in value over time; the freedom of practitioners from outside control over the practice of the profession; and the existence of associations that protect and promote the interest of the profession. There is also something referred to as a *service ideology*, which is the belief that the profession is of value or benefit to society. Occupations vary significantly in terms of the extent to which they are characterized by these features.

Art may be regarded as a profession because to one extent or another, it involves the following six occupational characteristics:

1. **Art involves long periods of training.** Although there may still be a few artists who succeed without a college education, most have at least a bachelor of fine arts degree and many have the master of fine arts degree, also. This educational background takes several years of training, possibly as much as four to six years beyond high school. In addition, proficiency in art takes continued practice and development to reach one's full occupational potential, making it similar to the length of training required of nurses, accountants, engineers, and public school teachers.

2. **Art training requires learning more than skills and techniques.** Artists also must be familiar with a wide range of ideas related to the important theoretical aspects of the visual arts. The interesting paradox is that art that is fundamentally conceptual may be represented visually only by the physical properties of the artist's material. Artists must learn not only the history and theory of art but also most of the same academic subject matter that is part of any undergraduate professional program. Traditional academic subjects such as literature, philosophy, and history may be a valuable source of artistic ideas.

3. **Artwork involves individual creativity, and artists must be allowed to develop their own ideas in environments that are cre-**

atively stimulating. Creativity develops only when artists are able to pursue their own ideas without intrusion or interference from others. This is why artists value their independence so highly—they may be encouraged to work, but they can't be forced to produce good art. Even graphic designers and illustrators employed by companies who work according to the specifications of clients must rely on their own creativity to translate those requirements into concrete ideas and images.

4. **There are several organizations and associations that exist to promote the interests of the professionals they serve.** Graphic designers, interior designers, art directors, publication designers, typographers, lithographers, and illustrators, for example, specify guidelines for the assessment of educational programs; set standards for professional conduct; promote testing for technical competency; establish guidelines for contracts; and promote a variety of educational, advocacy, and professional service activities. Although the fine art disciplines are not organized into associations that have the same kind of mandate, there are organizations and foundations that promote a variety of funding and support activities for the arts. Professional associations, organizations, and foundations for both the fine and applied arts may be found in the Appendix.

5. **Professions are distinguished from other occupations by the fact that they claim to provide services that are valuable to society.** Fine art provides a number of important benefits: it can symbolize and express social values, it can help establish and even promote useful patterns of cultural change, and it can serve as a basis for the development of a cultural identity. The applied arts by definition produce a concrete benefit to society. In addition to promoting benefits of direct practical value, they also can make essentially the same kind of social and cultural contributions as the fine

arts do. The social and cultural significance of art is important because it is assumed to be related to its market value.

6. Professions are characterized by the significant distinction between a job and a career. A job remains relatively static over time, not growing or changing in any way that increases the occupational knowledge, skills, and value of the worker. A career, by contrast, is characterized by occupational growth and development. Because an artist's occupational worth has the potential for continual expansion, art has the dynamic qualities of a career rather than the static characteristics of a job. The developmental nature of a career may be reflected by an increase in the quality of an artist's work over time and also by an increase in an artist's earning potential.

As mentioned earlier, it is important to remember that a career in art provides other satisfactions aside from providing a means to earning a good living. If you hope to become an artist, you must understand that the requirements of the profession are long periods of training that involve both a technical and theoretical component, and working independently without interference. You should also be prepared to address the role of art in satisfying some of the basic needs of society. If you are comfortable with these professional characteristics and have the talent to round out the equation, art may be a satisfying career choice.

Two Traditions in Art

In the last chapter you learned that there are two basic theories of art, one as a means to express individual creativity and the other as satisfying some basic functional needs. In reality these two ideas are woven together. Art that is primarily expressive may also have some potential to satisfy practical social needs, and art that is primarily useful in its purpose will probably also be produced in a way that expresses the individual creativity of the artist. This important point says something fundamental about art as an occupation— even when art is devoted purely to aesthetic objectives, it can have a practical side, and useful art can also be produced with some concern for beauty.

When you consider art as a profession, you will want to keep in mind the two broad categories that we mentioned in Chapter 1: art that is primarily concerned with individual creative expression and aesthetics is called *fine art*, and art that is produced largely for practical reasons is typically referred to as *applied art*. All art is essentially divided along these lines, and each professional area occupies its own niche in the art world. The distinction between the fine and applied arts begins in art school and extends into a full range of areas, including the art market, art publications, and professional organizations.

Fine Arts

Fine art is sometimes classified on the basis of such traditional media as oil or acrylic paint (painting), pencil (drawing), and stone or metal (sculpture). Additional media, including film, printmaking, photography, and the electronic arts such as video and computer art, form the basis for the remaining classifications of fine art.

Although each of these areas can fully exist on its own, fine art also includes mixed media, which is interdisciplinary in its approach and combines materials or techniques from more than one medium. The wall-mounted works of Elizabeth Murray or Frank Stella seem to combine both painting and sculpture. Some of the photography of William Beckley contains as much drawing and written text as it does photographic images. Almost any art medium you can think of has been combined with additional media to produce lively and imaginative works. Many contemporary mixed media works are composed of nontraditional material, such as plastic, resin, fabric, wood, concrete, and wire. Sometimes these materials are used in combination with either traditional art material or with manufactured products.

Fine art may be classified in other ways, also. One is based on the extent to which the work is either an abstract or a figurative representation of the real world. In a sense all art is abstract because a representation of something is not the same as the thing itself. The job of the artist is to translate the thing into an image. But taken to its extreme, the distinction between abstract and representational art is based on the viewer's ability to recognize the work as something that one can see.

A number of contemporary artists believe that distinctions based on media are irrelevant to what their work strives to achieve, and they would argue that distinctions should instead be based on the content or meaning of the work. So art may represent the artist's ideas and concepts, emotional life, political convictions, or concerns for formal aesthetic properties. These various interests and concerns are often integrated in an artist's work.

Other distinctions may be based on a particular style that is common to artists working in roughly the same time period, leading to such classifications as abstract impressionism, cubism, or postmodernism, for example. The influence of common cultural factors may have an impact on artists who have experienced their historical contexts in similar ways, thus producing a distinctive approach to art.

So fine art may be differentiated in a variety of ways, depending on the purposes of those who are making the distinctions. Fine art may be classified according to media (painting, printmaking, or digital); according to the aesthetic approach of the artist (abstract, representational, conceptual, or symbolic); and according to style (cubism, pointillism, or expressionism). These are some of the more common categories, but they are not the only ones. They are mentioned here because the approaches to art that they suggest are closely tied to the economic realities of the art market. Anyone who makes a living in fine art will very soon come to realize that the art market—the buying and selling of art—is to a large extent driven by changes in taste on the part of the art-buying public. This is just as true in the fields of applied art as it is in fine art.

Applied Arts

The other basic approach to art as a profession is the applied arts. Work produced in this tradition has a useful application and is therefore sometimes called *commercial art*. As we have seen, however, that term is not favored in the art world.

The largest area in the applied arts is design. This broad field includes advertising design, fashion design, graphic design, and interior design. There is even an art college in Los Angeles that offers a degree program in toy design. These design areas share a creative process that produces useful end results. Fashion designers, for example, create different styles of clothing. Graphic designers create page layouts, book covers, and company logos, as well as the designs for cereal boxes and other consumer packaging. Interior designers create safe, comfortable, and aesthetically satisfying spaces in which people can live, work, and play.

Illustration is an especially important example of an applied art that can be created in many styles. Illustration sometimes looks similar to representational fine art and typically involves the use of drawings or paintings that represent an idea, feeling, or message. Magazines often use illustrations to accompany stories or articles. Illustrations are also found in textbooks, children's books, brochures, catalogs, billboards, newspapers, product packaging, and advertising of all kinds.

Cartooning is an interesting applied art that is sometimes considered to be a kind of illustration. Cartoons are used more widely than is sometimes realized, appearing not only in comic books but also in package design, political cartoons, advertising, books, magazines, and public service messages.

The medium of photography is used to produce both fine and applied art, but its applied-art applications are perhaps the most pervasive and widely recognized. Applied photography is used in books, magazines, newspapers, brochures and catalogs, on billboards, and in political campaigns. It is especially important in print advertising of all kinds. Advertisers are well aware of the familiar aphorism that a picture is worth a thousand words; however, when pictures are combined with words, the result can produce an even more compelling effect.

Two other important areas of applied art are art education and art therapy, both of which focus more on the significance of the art-making process than the works themselves. Art education involves the teaching of art from kindergarten through the twelfth grade. In most public school systems and many private schools, art is considered an important part of the curriculum. It is thought to promote students' creative and imaginative abilities and introduce them to a basic hands-on art appreciation experience.

Art therapy also focuses on process more than product. This applied field is based on the expectation that individuals with a variety of physical and/or emotional problems may benefit from the personally enriching process of creating art. Most people believe that art enables people of any age to express feelings that would otherwise be blocked. Art therapists work in a variety of settings, but they are most often found in psychiatric, general, and Veterans Administration hospitals.

Finding a Balance

Professionals in some areas of art are typically employed by a company. These areas include art education or art therapy, interior design, and graphic design. Employers may include schools, publishing companies, advertising firms, or graphic design and interior design companies.

Professionals in these fields work for one employer at a time doing a basic type of work or a range of related kinds of tasks. This does not mean that their work is not creative and unique but that it is performed within a specific setting and schedule. We will discuss this type of employment further in subsequent chapters. At this point we will consider those artists who work independently.

Many artists and designers are self-employed. Fine artists are really very much like independent businesspeople, producing their own works and selling them in galleries. They also may receive funding through government grants for artists. Some designers also work for themselves. In fact, most people who work in photography or illustration do so as freelancers, and many people who work in fashion design or interior design freelance, also.

Working on a freelance basis, however, is a double-edged sword. Self-employment is a dream of many people, regardless of what their profession may be. It is ideal for those who can handle the rewards and responsibilities of working independently and who are able to sell their art or design work to clients who are willing to pay for their services. Nonetheless, freelancers in every field face times of frustration and doubt when business is slow and clients are scarce. Until you have built up a sufficient client list so that you can maintain some positive cash flow even in slow periods, you may very well experience times when you will need to look for alternate sources of income.

This doesn't necessarily have to be negative, however. Alternate sources of income may be just as satisfying as the art or design work itself. Many artists and designers work at any number of interesting and well-paying jobs, including positions as gallery directors, art teachers, or account executives for design firms. It may also mean that in the very early stages of your career, you may have to work at jobs that don't have a great deal of glamour or earning potential until you find your niche in the art world. This means that you may need to be prepared to wear two hats during the early part of your career. One will enable you to pay the rent; the other will allow you to produce your art.

A Career in Art

Art as a career is unlike most other professions, and you should have a clear sense of what makes it so distinctive. Simply put, art is something that creative individuals feel compelled to do. This may not be easy to understand for people who are strictly pragmatic and who view earning a living as the primary means of pursuing life's goals. For them, the means of achieving this objective are often secondary.

Artists have a different viewpoint, because their primary motivation is the creative process and the desire to produce art. However, creative self-actualization must be balanced with a concern for economic reality. Thus, artists need to be as concerned with the practical issues related to their careers as they are with issues of self-expression, finding a way to lead a creative yet balanced and productive professional life.

A Final Thought

In this chapter you learned about the characteristics of art that make it a profession. You have also seen that you may choose to work as either a fine artist or an applied artist, depending on whether you want your work to express individual creativity or to meet a basic functional need. Your personality and needs will play a role in determining which type of career you pursue—whether you are better suited to working for an employer or striking out on your own as a freelance artist.

4

CAREERS IN FINE ART

THE FIVE TRADITIONAL kinds of fine art—drawing, painting, sculpture, printmaking, and photography—are traditionally represented in art museums and galleries more often than in other media. However, more and more interesting and exciting work is being produced through computer art, video, ceramics, glassmaking, and fiber art. Artists will often work in several of these media throughout their careers, and they may move back and forth among them. Some combine media to such an extent that it is not always easy to classify a work according to materials or production.

Artists who work in the various fine art disciplines have a great deal in common from an occupational point of view. One distinguishing characteristic of fine artists is that they work alone, unlike other professionals whose work involves interaction with specific clients or segments of the population. In addition, most of these other professionals work in institutional settings, involving ongoing relationships with a wide range of colleagues and staff. Fine artists, by contrast, generally work without much assistance, advice, or consultation from anyone.

Perhaps the most central fact of economic life for fine artists is that they produce work for which there is no specific ready-made market. The basic problem for all artists is getting their art into the art market and having it accepted by the buying public. Actually, these two economic issues are very much interrelated.

Gallery System

Galleries lie at the heart of the art market. They are where artists exhibit and sell their work and are essentially boutiques or specialty stores that specialize in selling art. Depending on the size of the artwork and the amount of available space, a gallery may have as few as ten or as many as two hundred or more pieces of art at any time.

Artists usually begin to exhibit or show their work while they are in art school. These shows give students the experience of presenting work to a public audience and establish the foundation for their résumés. Graduate school can offer students additional opportunities for gallery exposure. Other possibilities include art competitions, as well as city or regional art programs that bring art to the public. Competitions enable students to submit their work and have it evaluated by a jury. These competitions may lead to honors, cash prizes, or exhibitions.

In order to sell art, however, an artist must find a gallery that is willing to show it. How do galleries learn about the work of up-and-coming artists? Some are willing to look at photographic slides of an artist's work, but this is not a particularly efficient way to have your work taken seriously by a gallery dealer and accepted for a show. This is especially true in a large city like New York or Toronto, where many artists are working and dealers can be selective. Dealers in smaller cities may be more likely to accept an artist based on slides and portfolios.

Another way to reach the art-buying public is through artists' cooperatives, which are galleries run by artists who pay a fee to rent space and show their work. This enables artists to pay for gallery exposure until they are able to establish contact with a dealer who is willing to accept their work. Although the exposure is valuable, cooperatives require a great deal of time and energy because, in addition to paying rent, artists must handle such administrative chores as maintaining the gallery space, scheduling shows, and staffing the facility. Also, showing in a cooperative gallery is often based more on financial resources than artistic ability. Co-ops generally exist at the lower end of the highly stratified gallery hierarchy.

It is more common for an artist to be introduced to a dealer through another artist or someone else connected to the gallery. This makes networking a very important way of getting to know people who have contacts in the art world. Artists who have nearly completed art school or have recently graduated may be introduced to dealers by their teachers. This is just one of several reasons why it is important to attend an art college with faculty who are themselves active professional artists. Your teachers may be able to help you to make important professional contacts in both undergraduate and graduate degree programs. These contacts may prove to be invaluable.

A gallery will either select one or two pieces of an artist's work as part of a group show, or it may have a solo exhibition featuring the work of a single artist. Both types of exhibits are important because they present the work to the buying public. While any exposure is valuable, a solo show carries more prestige for the artist and is, therefore, a better vehicle for selling work and developing a reputation. This does not mean that group shows aren't valuable; some can have an extremely important impact on an artist's reputation, based on the venue and the show's history.

Showing work in a gallery accomplishes two crucial things—it exposes the artist's work to the buying public, and it validates the worth of the work in the eyes of prospective buyers. The issue from a marketing point of view is that gallery exposure can influence the perceptions of people who see the work.

It is obvious that having work accepted by a gallery will be an important part of developing your career, but there is also another issue to consider. An artist's work is judged, in part, by the quality of the gallery in which it appears. Galleries are hierarchically ranked in terms of reputation and prestige. Those with strong reputations will increase the value of the art they show, while those with weaker reputations will call the value of the art they show into question. It is important to have your first few shows in a good gallery, which will set the stage for subsequent evaluations by dealers who will want to know where your work has been shown.

Another concern is finding a gallery whose dealer has compatible aesthetic sensibilities. This is less important in smaller cities, where galleries tend to generalize and will exhibit an eclectic array of work. Galleries in larger cities, on the other hand, usually specialize in particular kinds of art. Artists ideally like to show work in galleries that have a solid reputation and are known for promoting work they find compatible with their own. The key is to establish visibility in a credible and compatible gallery context.

Galleries sell artwork for a commission and will typically take 50 percent of the price of each sale. Because this is a business, artists and dealers have a highly interdependent yet sometimes strained relationship. They cannot do without each other, yet each may feel as though his or her contribution has greater value in the relationship. To avoid the potential problems that artists sometimes face in dealing with galleries, it is important to find a dealer with whom you can establish a good relationship. Avoiding personality conflicts can go a long way toward resolving problems before they occur.

The best way for an artist to avoid problems is to conduct relationships with gallery dealers using standard business practices. This means using signed contracts for all transactions between the artists and dealers. There are a variety of contracts covering different kinds of professional relationships with galleries, including consignment agreements, exclusive contracts, and monthly allowances against total sales. An understanding must be reached on matters such as when payment for sales will be made, who absorbs courtesy discounts for large purchases, and any out-of-gallery sales. Many useful guides to handling the business side of art and design are listed under Recommended Reading at the end of the book.

There is one other matter that can cause tension between artists and dealers. Because there is a relationship between the artistic product and the marketability of the work, some dealers make suggestions about such creative matters as the size, materials, or content of an artist's work. Artists vary in their responses to this kind of input. Those who place particular emphasis on selling their work may be receptive to suggestions from dealers who know what sells. Other artists are not inclined to accept such suggestions. In either case, the primary responsibility of the artist in relations with gallery dealers will be maintaining the quality of artistic production.

Specialized Galleries

Specialization gives galleries a distinctive position in the art market. There are a number of ways they can specialize, such as selling work from a particular historical period or, in the case of contemporary art, representing the artistic taste or vision of the dealer. But galleries also can specialize in the medium used to create the work, such as photography or sculpture.

Other galleries specialize in work that has traditionally been recognized as craft. These works are primarily defined by utilitarian or practical purposes and are created using traditional methods and materials. Typical examples of craft works include useful objects made of ceramics, glass, and fiber. In recent years, these methods and materials have been used to create works that are not primarily utilitarian in value but are singular in design, are created for the same expressive and aesthetic reasons as paintings or sculpture, and may cost many thousands of dollars. In such cases, craft work should really be regarded as art.

It may not always be easy, however, to tell whether a piece of work is art or craft. Consider a glass vase that is made by hand and costs $500. If the artist's intention was for it to be used as a vase, then its usefulness may define it as craft work. But what about a unique handmade vase that costs $15,000 and is displayed as a piece of sculpture in a museum or executive office? This would be defined by its aesthetic value rather than by its potential practical value. Also, if people were to think of it as a piece of "art," then by that definition it would have to be regarded as art. As discussed in Chapter 1, if this question is viewed from a sociological point of view, then art is whatever people and social institutions define it as being. The more difficult examples to define would be those works that are an ambiguous mix of practicality and beauty.

Just as there is a hierarchy of galleries for traditional art, there is a hierarchy for ceramics, glass, and fiber as well. There are fewer galleries that specialize only in the highest quality work in these media than those that deal in fine art, but recognition of this work is growing. There are many more outlets for works that sell at a more modest price. Some of these outlets also include gift shops, museum shops, furniture stores, accessory shops, and annual craft fairs. Works at the lower end of the price scale are much more likely to be regarded as crafts in the traditional sense of the term.

Online Galleries

The Internet is an ever growing source of art sales. Online galleries vary in the quality of the work they offer. Some sell the work of established artists with strong reputations as well as emerging artists who are beginning to establish themselves. These galleries offer a wide range of work including photography, painting, sculpture, film, textile, and mixed media.

Online galleries provide a number of services for customers. The obvious advantage is that they allow viewers to look at the work of different artists from the comfort of their home or office. But they also provide biographical information about the artists as well as basic information about art concepts and terminology.

Other online services provide information about galleries, dealers, and museums in various cities around the United States and Canada. These websites offer information about the artists who are represented, the dates of exhibitions, and the style or genre in which the gallery or museum might specialize. A Web search for art galleries will lead to many options for you to explore.

Art Museums

Galleries generally sell the work of artists but do not collect it. Museums, by contrast, will buy the work of artists and keep it in their collections.

A museum will typically acquire the work of an artist in one of four ways:

1. The museum curator may learn about an up-and-coming artist, perhaps through a positive review of a show, and buy a work directly from a gallery for the museum's collection.

2. A curator may actively look for new artists or for artists who are doing a particular kind of work the museum wants to acquire. The curator will then comb the galleries for new work to buy.

3. An art collector may donate a piece to a museum to help enhance an artist's reputation or as a tax-deductible contribution.

4. An artist may donate a piece of his or her work to a museum. However, a museum will take only the best of what is offered and will carefully screen the artist's work in order to maintain its own reputation.

Having work accepted by a museum is a major step in an artist's career, one that relatively few artists achieve. Just as there is a hierarchy among galleries, there is also a hierarchy among museums. In North America, the most important museums are usually in major cities, but many small cities have fine museums as well.

The significance of having work in a museum collection depends in part on the reputation of the museum, which should be assessed in the context of two economic systems. First, all work will be judged in terms of where it stands in relationship to the national and international art scene. Second, art is also judged in terms of where it stands within a particular art market. The purpose of an evaluation will determine the context for comparison.

It follows that the status and marketability of an artist's work will be affected by the reputation of the museum in which it is shown. A local artist's work that has been accepted by a museum in a small city may not stack up very well against the status and marketability of work by an internationally known artist in major museums in New York or Paris. Yet the more important point is that works of art find their own market levels and can contribute to the economic success and prestige of artists in a local as well as an international context.

Museums and their impact on the value of art may seem a long way off as you consider beginning a career in art. But successful artists are often discovered by important galleries and museums at relatively young ages, and many artists have achieved recognition in their twenties and thirties. It's important to remember, however, that most artists must at least get through undergraduate if not graduate art training before gaining prominence.

Art Consultants

Museums are not the only institutions that purchase art; many large and small businesses do as well. Small businesses need art for lobbies, reception areas, and offices. This art is generally bought by the company owner or an employee. If a company moves into a new space, an interior designer may acquire art for the new offices. In either case, the purchase is likely to be made by someone who is not a specialist in art.

However, there are consultants who specialize in purchasing art for companies. These professionals typically work for major corporations with large budgets, advising individuals or art selection committees who are responsible for the purchases. Corporations acquire art for a variety of reasons. They may want to place art in executive offices, meeting rooms, reception areas, and lobby spaces of company headquarters. Or a company may want to purchase art for their corporate collection as a means of showing visible support for the arts. Some companies, such as hotels, restaurant chains, and cruise lines, may need art as part of the interior design plan.

Art consultants may be employed by large interior design and architectural firms. These firms often provide a wide range of services to clients who need new or renovated office spaces. A large company that hires an architect to build a new headquarters or regional office may ask for help in purchasing art; a large architectural firm may have an in-house art consultant who may provide that service.

There are two fundamental approaches to purchasing art for corporations—it is either selected primarily for its decorative value or with a concern for its enduring artistic qualities. Art of the first kind is typically used to accent customer contact areas in restaurants, movie theaters, or hotels. Such art is typically not expensive and must be purchased with a concern for decorative issues such as color, size, and subject matter. Art of the second kind is generally purchased for corporate collections with a concern for investment value. The credentials and reputation of the artist are much more important in this case, which is where the knowledge and expertise of the art consultant becomes most useful.

When a company wants to build or add to its corporate art collection, it will hire a consultant who will be paid directly by the firm for services rendered. This contract is such an important aspect of the art consulting business that both the Association of Corporate Art Consultants and the Association of Professional Art Advisors have established guidelines for its use. One important stipulation states that consultants should not receive a percentage of the sale from the corporation, the artist, or the gallery from which the artwork is bought, which helps prevent the conflict of interest that might develop if a consultant's fee is tied to the dollar value of the sale.

An art consultant who has been hired to purchase valuable pieces will have a library of slides or digital images of the work of many artists. The consultant will show slides of several artists whose work might satisfy the client's requirements. Once the client selects a few possibilities, the consultant may show the actual artwork. When the final selections have been made, the purchase takes place through the consultant, who will buy the artwork on behalf of the client through a gallery that represents the artist or will purchase the art directly from the artist if that individual markets his or her work.

It is worth noting that corporate collections play a significant role in the art world. Most important, perhaps, is that their purchases of art provide a significant source of income for artists. In addition, corporate art collections serve to legitimize the art they hold. The works held in the collections of such major corporations as Microsoft, IBM, General Mills, and many others often have significant aesthetic and market value based on the knowledge and expertise of the art consultants who help shape the collections. It is, therefore, not surprising that corporate collections are often known for their quality. For this reason, artists' résumés will prominently display the names of corporate collections that have purchased their work.

Private Collectors

Private collectors play a major role in the art world, as their focused collections can consolidate and preserve disparate works of art that might not be brought together otherwise. They also can stimulate the development of the art they support through their patronage.

Collectors will purchase and hold works of art that they will either display or keep in storage. Their buying power allows them to have a great deal of impact on the art market, as well as direct economic impact on the artists themselves. The more work of a particular artist they buy, the more the perceived value of the artist grows.

The buying patterns of collectors typically fall into one of three categories. First, collectors who want to own the work of a hot new artist will purchase a single piece based solely on the artist's reputation. From the point of view of artists, this impromptu and rather unfocused manner of collecting is usually a momentary event in the economic life of an artist. Some of these collectors will purchase more than one work by a particular artist, however, and are naturally more important to the artist's career.

Second are those collectors who are building focused collections and who acquire a work because it makes a contribution to the theme of their collection. They may contribute to an artist's income and status because of the care, intelligence, and discrimination they use to build their collections.

The third kind of collector is even more focused, building a collection that is based on the work of one artist. This is perhaps the most coveted type of collector from the artist's point of view. Such collectors make ongoing commitments to the long-range value of the artists whose works they purchase. This type of relationship between artists and collectors may take on a personal as well as an economic dimension. In such cases, they will sometimes know one another personally and spend time with one another socially.

Art Styles and the Art Market

Some artists establish such strong reputations that the economic value of their work will transcend the vagaries of the art market. In most cases, these are deceased artists of such historical significance that their work will retain its value regardless of current trends. For living artists, however, the monetary value of their work is at least partly determined by its significance within the context of a market that is responsive to changing fashion and taste. In this way, the art market is subject to some of the same kinds of forces that affect the value of other commodities over time.

As trends in art change, the market value of certain styles or artists will also change. Sometimes an artist is very much in the center of things and then seems to fade from the scene, and art that is considered important at one time may become less popular later. This doesn't mean that art is as disposable as yesterday's hairstyle, but it does mean that the career of an artist over time may need to be responsive to the realities of changes in the art market.

Success is one force that can sometimes suppress artistic change. Artists who are able to sell their work may be reluctant to substantially alter what they produce. It is also true that gallery dealers thrive on consistency and are, therefore, leery about seeing their best artists move into new and uncharted territories. These factors can inhibit an artist's ability to move with or anticipate changing art currents.

In Chapter 2, we saw that artists will develop ideas until they are satisfied that they have explored as many aesthetic possibilities as the ideas allow. That desire for exploration and experimentation will push artists in new directions. This is an important driving force behind creativity, but it is not the only one. The realities of an ever-changing art market also have the potential to influence an artist's work, and few artists are indifferent to what sells and what does not. Such observations can have an impact on what artists perceive to be aesthetically satisfying in their own work. Not all artists are moved by such forces, but the potential for this type of influence is real. For sincere artists who want to sell their work, the challenge may be to balance artistic integrity with the economic reality of the public taste in art.

Market Value of Art

There are essentially two approaches to the issue of the value of art. One focuses on philosophical questions related to the relationship between art and human experience. From this point of view, the value of art is judged in terms of aesthetic qualities and their impact on people. Thus, art is judged to be valuable if it satisfies our need for aesthetic experience, gives us insight into the human condition, or promotes the cultural life of society.

From an economic point of view, however, the value of art is determined by what people are willing to pay for it. It is typically assumed, or at least hoped, that there is a positive relationship between the aesthetic quality of art and its price. Yet a basic question remains—how is the price determined?

Art prices are set by the gallery dealer and artist together. Although the price is arbitrary, it is influenced by a variety of factors, one of which is the subjective evaluation that the dealer and artist make of the quality of the art. This kind of judgment is based on experience and knowledge of the quality of other art with an established price.

Other more objective factors include the number and the importance of gallery shows the artist has had and the amount of money the artist's work has previously sold for. Of particular importance are the number and quality of reviews of the artist's work. The size of the artwork can also be a factor, since larger pieces generally sell for a higher price than smaller pieces by the same artist. All of this means that the price of art is determined by subjective perceptions and objective market factors.

Another significant consideration is the general economic climate during which art is sold, as well as the particular economic condition of the art market itself. During the 1980s, for example, art was considered to be a good economic investment. A lot of art was bought during that time with the expectation that its value would continue to rise. The value of the art did rise, but it rose beyond what the market could sustain. When people who bought at high prices tried to sell, they could not always do so, because buyers who realized that the market was overinflated either stayed away altogether or only bought work that had a more traditional appeal. Our current economic forecast is uncertain, with soaring fuel prices and a plunging housing market; it will be interesting to see what effect this climate has on the art market over the next few years.

Young artists who anticipate selling their first works may have unrealistically high expectations. An artist having a first gallery show and whose work is not known in the art community may have difficulty selling work for more than a few hundred to a few thousand dollars, depending on the prestige of the gallery and size of the city. The value of an artist's work, however, will increase gradually and often dramatically over time.

Economic Role of Critics

An art critic can influence the public's perception of the value of an artist's work in much the same way that a film critic can influence the perception of a movie. The important difference, however, is that most people will see a film they are interested in despite a critical review. The same is not necessarily true in the art world, where the people who pay attention to reviews are those who purchase the expensive works.

For one thing, taste is not the only factor to consider when purchasing art for a collection, as it might be when purchasing a single piece to hang in a living room. For serious collectors, art is not only something to be enjoyed but also something that has economic value that will either grow or diminish. These people want to be confident that the art they buy will increase or at least maintain its value. Moreover, some collectors purchase art exclusively as an investment. They will turn to art critics for an opinion, especially when an individual work costs many thousands of dollars.

Critics publish their opinions in magazines, newspapers, special art journals, and online. Those who work for major newspapers publish opinions that carry much weight, and journals such as *Art in America*, *Art Forum*, *ARTnews Magazine*, and *Art Papers* publish reviews that can be very important to the career of an artist. These journal reviews focus on work that is currently showing in galleries, so a strong review by a critic can add significantly to both the reputation and economic value of an artist's work. The New York artist William Beckley has speculated that one strong review in an important art journal may be worth as many as six or seven gallery exhibitions toward enhancing an artist's reputation.

Educational Credentials

The résumé is a very important part of an artist's overall marketing strategy because it assures gallery dealers and private collectors of the quality of the artist's work. But assessing that quality may be difficult because the evaluation criteria are not always clear, and the evaluation process is partly based on opinion. This is why an artist's gallery shows, reviews, and museum holdings are so important. Although they are also based on subjective perceptions, they provide independent evidence that others in the art world have acknowledged the significance of the artist's work.

An artist's educational background can also help to validate the subjective opinions of his or her art. The quality of the art school and degree earned are important because a strong educational background implies that an artist's work has developed out of a specific institutional tradition of knowledge, expertise, and artistic success. The substance of an artwork is expected to be associated with the educational credentials of the artist.

Grants and Other Funding Sources

Government funding is available for both young artists and those with established careers. The National Endowment for the Arts (NEA) and Canada Council for the Arts (CCA) are major sources of such funding. Both support regional organizations, such as the Southern Arts Federation and the Alberta Creative Development Initiative, as well as many other arts programs and institutions throughout North America that award grants to artists. Cities as well as state councils and commissions on the arts also make grants to artists.

There are a number of publications and websites that provide information about grants and other sources of support for artists. Some of these include the *NEA Guide* (www.nea.gov/pub), www.art deadlineslist.com, and www.absolutearts.com. Magazines such as *Art Week* and *Afterimage* also list funding sources for individual artists. *Art Calendar* is another useful periodical for announcements of juried art shows.

Another valuable resource that can provide information and referral to organizations is the Visual Artists Information Hotline, a program of the New York Foundation for the Arts. It provides information on funding, insurance, legal assistance, artists' colonies and residences, public art programs, and other services for artists. Visit www.nyfa.org/vaih for information.

Earnings

Earnings for fine artists vary depending on several factors, including the type of art they produce, their geographic location, and whether they are steadily employed or working on a freelance basis.

Fine artists have median annual earnings of about $42,000. The majority earn between $29,000 and $59,000; while the lowest paid earn about $20,000 and the highest paid earn more than $80,000.

It is important to realize that only some fine artists make a living exclusively from the sale of their works, especially at the early stages of their careers. When planning a career in art, it's a good idea to anticipate the prospect of finding alternative sources of income. Although it might initially seem frustrating to need to develop a contingency plan, it doesn't have to be negative. Many alternative sources of income may be a satisfying part of a flexible professional career. For instance, teaching is one of the most important and gratifying ways that an artist can find to support a budding career because this is an opportunity to earn a living while sharing knowledge and continuing to learn from colleagues.

Fine artists may find some occupational flexibility by working in both the fine and applied art areas. For example, painters may do illustration or photography. Fine art photographers may do freelance work as applied-art photographers. Fine artists with a background in graphic design may find work in that area. There are many career-enhancing possibilities for imaginative and entrepreneurial artists. An open mind and resourceful attitude will be valuable for any artist who seeks to take advantage of available opportunities.

A Final Thought

You now have an idea of how a career in fine arts might proceed and an understanding of the art market and how the value of art is estimated. Galleries, private collectors, and museums are all potential markets for visual artists, and a strong résumé will help you to promote your work in each of these areas. Commitment to your work combined with a strong educational foundation and a realistic approach to the financial possibilities will provide a solid basis for beginning a career in the fine arts.

5

CAREERS IN DESIGN COMPANIES

DESIGN COMPANIES ARE, in a way, human service organizations. Although they produce a finished product, their real function is to help clients resolve a problem or satisfy a need—which places a full range of demands on the artist's technical, personal, and communication skills.

Artists and designers must be able to understand their clients' needs and convey ideas about how those needs may be addressed through particular design solutions. Those who are employed by design companies and the design departments of large corporations must be able to work as part of a team, with each member contributing his or her special skill, knowledge, and expertise to the design project. This system also places demands on the designer's ability to work effectively with people in an institutional context.

Some artists and designers may not feel comfortable working in these complex social environments, preferring the relative independence of freelance work. However, even the most individualistic and free-spirited person will probably need to spend at least some time working in an organizational setting. Until an artist has built a portfolio of professional work, getting freelance work will not be easy. Also, even though art schools do an excellent job preparing students to enter the world of work, they cannot teach them all of the important tricks of the trade that come from years of experience. Working for a design firm for at least a few years may place the young artist or designer in the company of seasoned professionals who can provide valuable on-the-job training.

This chapter will cover four basic areas of art and design: graphic design, advertising design, interior design, and fashion design. These areas cover a wide range of occupational experiences that can be extrapolated to other career areas.

Graphic Design

Graphic design includes a variety of specializations, such as book design, magazine design, logo design, package design, typography, digital animation, and motion graphics. Unlike illustration or fine art areas such as painting, in which artists work alone on projects, graphic design involves a number of different people whose creative talents and activities are integrated into a common team effort.

Graphic designers may be asked to design page layouts for a magazine, a company logo, a system of informational signs for the interior of an organization (environmental design), a brochure, a shopping bag, banners, labels for consumer products, trade show graphics and displays, CD or DVD covers, restaurant menus, a company's annual report, packaging for a new product, or web pages. A major task of graphic designers is to design the layout of the printed page. This involves organizing the text or copy, selecting the lettering, and arranging any photographs or illustrations on a page. Page layout is done for magazines, books, brochures, newsletters, and pamphlets.

Design Process

The first phase of the design project for any job begins with the client, whose needs will be established in an initial meeting. In general, the client will want the designer to call attention to either a product or a service or to organize information or other printed matter.

How the designer proceeds with the job will depend on a number of factors. The designer must be aware of such things as the demographic characteristics of the customers or users of the clients' services, the tastes or preferences of those customers, the design approach of the clients' competitors, and the specific style trends related to colors, images, shapes, and so forth. Experienced designers may already be familiar with some of this important background information, but some research will most likely be required.

After these initial discussions, the designer should have a clear idea of what the client needs. A series of meetings will then take place at the design studio to determine what specific talents and skills the design team will need to complete the project. In addition to one or more graphic designers, for example, the team may require a photographer, a writer to prepare copy, and a typographer to style lettering.

The initial round of meetings will focus primarily on developing ideas. The designer may prepare a number of preliminary sketches to work out some basic design ideas. The team's creative director will then take the best design ideas and have them developed into somewhat more detailed preproduction drawings called *comps* ("comprehensive" representations of the basic design ideas).

The drawings will go through a series of stages, including thumbnail comps, marker comps, and electric printout comprehensives.

When the designer is satisfied with the ideas that have been developed, a finished or presentation comp is prepared and shown to the client for feedback. It is possible that this first comp won't be acceptable to the client, and the process must be continued until the team comes up with one that the client will approve. At that point, the process will move forward to production. Now the designer becomes responsible for more than the basic design but also for the budget and schedule, as well as the production specifications of the project. If a pamphlet or brochure is being prepared, the designer will take bids and hire a printer. The designer also will have to select the color and weight of the paper and the color of the ink used in printing. All of this is done with a series of predetermined deadlines.

The final phase of the design process occurs when digital files, which consist of written copy, artwork, and typography, are prepared and sent to the printer. At this point, PDFs or "brown line" or "blue line" contact prints are made from the digital files and are checked for any errors. This is a critical step because the public will see the final product, and errors may be embarrassing and costly for all concerned. The design work is then ready for printing.

Organization of Design

There is as much variation in the basic staff makeup of design companies as there is in the various phases of the design process. There are three fundamental things to know about design organizations. First, much design work is done either in design firms or in the design departments of large corporations. Design firms are specialty companies that provide design work for other businesses that require their services.

The work of design companies generally focuses on the needs that a client company wishes to communicate with its customers or clients. Some work of this nature may be perceived as relatively glamorous, especially when the design work increases the client's ability to earn income, has a high level of visual appeal, and has the potential to reach a large audience. Such projects may significantly enhance the reputation of the designer, particularly any work that is associated with package design for products or web pages that are well known or for other kinds of national campaigns. Designers often gain prestige and recognition from client companies that have a high degree of visibility or that are widely familiar.

By contrast, much of the work that is done by the design department of a large corporation is focused on in-house needs. Internal publications, such as newsletters, training manuals, and corporate reports, are usually handled by the in-house design department. In addition, this department will typically handle new applications for existing designs. This might entail making use of an existing package design for a new company product or making some modifications to an established package design. In either case, the designer will be responsible for working with an existing design rather than creating and developing a completely new concept. When the company decides to embark on a major design overhaul of its packaging or company logo, an outside design firm is often brought in to handle this specialized assignment.

This means that work done by an in-house design department is not always the most creative or glamorous, but the corporate pay structure may offer attractive salaries and benefits for starting designers. Salaries will vary depending on the size of the company and the region of the country where it is located. Another benefit of starting a career in a design department is that large corporate budgets often permit departments to purchase the best available material and equipment. Working with state-of-the-art professional equipment may be a valuable experience for a young designer. Moreover, working for a large corporation with a high degree of visibility or name recognition can add considerably to a designer's résumé and portfolio.

Second, design companies will either specialize in a particular type of design work or will provide a more general range of design services. To some extent this will depend on the size of the city in which the design company is located. In New York, where there is a flourishing market for design, it is possible for a company to specialize in two-dimensional or "flat" design work, which involves the kind of graphic design that might be seen in magazines, websites, or on compact discs. Or it may be possible for a company to specialize in three-dimensional work, such as package design or exhibition design.

In both large and small cities, many companies are likely to do a variety of types of design work. Especially in a slow economic period, few companies will be in a position to turn work away. Moreover, some projects require the use of more than one discipline. An interior design project, for example, may include interior architecture, lighting design, and environmental graphics (location signs and directions). Therefore, students in art school would be well advised to get as broad a design education as they can in order to increase their versatility and thus their attractiveness to prospective employers.

There are advantages to working in either kind of design firm. On the one hand, specialized firms can give designers valuable expertise in an area for which there is proven demand. On the other hand, the design generalist will have a more flexible range of skills and knowledge to offer a prospective employer. In the final analysis, a young designer's future may be more the result of a combination of luck, rational planning, and career management.

Design work occurs in a variety of other institutional settings as well. These include department stores, newspapers, television and film studios, record companies, magazines, publishers, computer companies, marketing firms, public relations firms, and museums. Designers in these organizations work in situations much like those of in-house design departments. A major difference, however, is that the work they produce is much more likely to reach the public.

Third, design companies vary in size. A small company may have as few as three or four employees, not including freelance designers who work on their own. A large firm may have more than one hundred people on staff.

Consider the division of labor in a mid-size firm of thirty people. About one-third of the staff will be designers. There will also be a president and vice president (who may be designers, copywriters, or marketing specialists, or have another valuable skill related to design), a creative director, a few copywriters, perhaps three or four salespersons, an administrative assistant, and a receptionist. In addition, any number of freelance artists may be brought in on particular projects. These freelancers might include a photographer, a typographer, or an illustrator.

Basic Areas of Responsibility

The tasks of designers essentially fall into two broad categories. First, they must create design ideas that communicate, inform, instruct, and influence. This means that they must think about how a product, service, or idea should be represented visually. Since contemporary society is flooded with visual clutter, however, the key is to present the idea in a way that will catch the public's attention. This is no easy task, to create an image and text that will arrest the eye and stimulate the mind. It takes a creative and imaginative person to accomplish this, and that creativity is what separates good designers from merely capable ones.

Second, designers must have the technical proficiency necessary to translate their ideas into a finished product that can be sent to production. The graphic designers will handle a number of very specific tasks. One important job—one that is actually a specialization for some designers—involves making *marker comps*. This refers to drawings of people or products in situations. They are made with a felt-tipped marker and are used to represent in rough form what the final design might look like. These drawings are not at all sophisticated or refined in a technical sense; in fact, they often have a rather childlike or stick-figure quality. Their value, however, is that they can effectively communicate design concepts to a client or other members of the design team. In later stages of the design process, more sophisticated and technically complete comps will be prepared until a final production comp is made ready for printing.

It is also crucial that designers have good language skills and be able to get along well with other people—an ability to communicate visually is not enough. Designers are often engaged in a social environment that involves interaction with clients, members of their design team, technical support staff, suppliers, and production people. In addition, they must write memos, reports, e-mails, and business letters in a lucid manner. On occasion, designers may also be called upon to write copy for the work being designed.

Computers

Computers are the standard design tool and are used to produce nearly all phases of design work. This means that designers may bring together the diverse parts of a project, including images and written copy, and assemble them on the computer screen. The images, copy, background, and other design elements may be moved around quickly and easily, allowing designers to work more efficiently in terms of time and money. Before computers, for example, changing the typeface on a page layout was costly and took a good deal of time, whereas now computers make it possible to experiment with dozens of type styles in a matter of minutes.

The ability to manipulate the various elements with such speed also makes it easier to experiment with design variations. Once an initial design has been selected, the computer may be used to make comps that will show clients what the final product will actually look like. Since these computer-generated comps can be redesigned quickly, it is possible to make a client's changes immediately, resulting in a more rapid approval of the design.

Computers are used in graphic design and advertising design because they enable work to be finished quickly and therefore inexpensively. Publishing, in particular, has been more affected by the use of computers for graphic design than any other area. The speed with which design work may be done is of primary importance. Designers now do page layouts for a magazine in a fraction of the time it used to take.

Computers are also used in the production phase of the process. It is possible, for example, to use the computer to actually make the mechanicals that go to the printer. A few graphic design companies still make mechanicals by hand, but most are now using the computer. In fact, some design firms will simply transfer their final design work by modem through the telephone line or cable to the printer for final processing.

A great deal of design work is also necessary for the Internet. All companies with websites use designers to integrate images and text. Websites often employ motion graphics to add movement to their pages. This makes websites more interesting and potentially more attractive and informative.

Earnings

According to the American Institute of Graphic Arts, the median annual total cash compensation for entry-level designers was $35,000 in 2007. Staff-level graphic designers earned a median of $45,000. Senior designers, who may supervise junior staff or have some decision-making authority that reflects their knowledge of graphic design, earned a median of $62,000.

Solo designers who freelanced or worked under contract for another company reported median earnings of $60,000.

Design directors—the creative heads of design firms or in-house corporate design departments—earned $98,600. Graphic designers with ownership or partnership interests in a firm or who were principals of the firm in some other capacity earned $113,000.

Advertising Design

Advertising design involves a team effort that integrates the talents of a variety of people, making this a professional field for those who not only think creatively but who also are able to work cooperatively with other people. Perhaps as much as any of the applied arts, success in advertising requires designers to be sensitive to the cultural themes that they reveal through their ads. Those cultural nuances are what enable advertising designers to convey a visual language with which their target audience can identify.

Size of Agencies

Most advertising is created in ad agencies. The size of an agency is usually measured by their "billings" (total amount of revenues) each year. A small agency will have less than $100 million in billings, while a large agency handles $100 million or more. The basic creative team in any size agency will typically include a creative director (the senior-level person most responsible for the work that the agency does), art directors (who come up with the advertising ideas and create comps), copywriters (who write the words in an advertisement and may be involved in developing basic ideas for the ad campaign), and studio artists (who prepare the layouts and mechanicals for the final copy of the ad). In addition, there may be junior art directors and junior copywriters who are asked to handle smaller accounts.

A large agency with a complete staff may also employ graphic designers, typographers, and video specialists. Many agencies, however, will hire illustrators and photographers on a freelance basis to do special assignments that are not handled routinely by the agency. As with other design fields, these various technical disciplines become integrated through digital applications. Small agencies, in particular, may not have a large enough volume of work to permanently employ certain kinds of staff, but large agencies hire temporary specialists as well. An ad agency will hire freelance specialists depending on whether the capabilities of the in-house staff are adequate for the technical requirements of a particular job.

Advertising covers a lot of territory. It includes everything from the sign announcing a local high school's fund-raiser car wash to the multimillion dollar ad campaigns that are handled by the world's largest agencies. For example, a relatively small advertising job that involves creating an ad for a clothing store to be run in a local newspaper might be given either to an ad agency or to a graphic design studio. Larger companies with a local or regional focus will work with ad agencies that handle advertising for those markets. But the advertising for major national corporations belongs exclusively to the large and prestigious advertising agencies.

These agencies handle in excess of $100 million in annual billings and are responsible for all of the advertising that you see on national television and in major national magazines. Most of the clients are companies that sell consumer products ranging from cars to pet food to computers to soft drinks and just about anything else you can think of. These are the agencies that design the ads you see everywhere from newspaper advertising supplements to the Super Bowl television commercials.

In addition, there are large companies such as the General Electric Corporation that sell many consumer products but that also want to have "goodwill" advertising for the company as a whole. Such advertising may be part of a public relations strategy to maintain the trust and goodwill of the public. Major corporations that sell business-to-business products and services may also use advertising as part of a public relations effort. Advertising may, therefore, pursue a variety of objectives.

Ad Campaigns

To create an ad campaign, an agency must develop a single message or set of messages that are intended to achieve a limited range of objectives through advertising. The messages are usually simple and straightforward: Volvos are safe cars, Bounty paper towels are durable, Verizon Wireless service offers extensive support. Some campaigns include a set of related messages that are either implicit or explicit. Commercials for safe driving that are produced for a beer company, for example, may convey a message that explicitly promotes the idea that one should never drive under the influence of alcohol, but that also implies that the beer company is civic-minded and responsive to the needs of the community.

The campaign also will use a basic message or set of messages in a series of specific advertisements that may appear over a period of time. The ads may go through stages that develop different aspects of a message or that reinforce the message by repeating a familiar advertising idea or approach. Some of these campaigns become advertising icons. The "priceless" ads designed for MasterCard are an example of an approach that remains fresh in spite of its repeated use. Many ad campaigns use celebrities either as on-screen pitchmen or to supply voiceover narration. James Earl Jones is synonymous with Verizon, and Donald Sutherland reminds us that Simply Orange is fresh juice.

An ad campaign can also promote a basic message by using an idea in more than one advertising medium. Nike products, for example, may use Michael Jordan in television, magazine, and point-of-sales advertising. This allows the company to reach its target audience in more than one way, enabling the advertisements in a variety of media to reinforce one another.

An agency begins an advertising assignment by formulating a creative work plan. This plan will focus on the business objective of the client; what action the company wants people to take with respect to their product (to buy it at a store, call for printed information, or order it online); the message the company wants to tell its customers; what distinctive benefit the product offers; the demographic characteristics of the customers the ad will target; and information about their preferences and what kind of visual images they will respond to.

Getting a Start

The creative side of advertising is an attractive work setting for young people, with good reason. The world of advertising is fast-paced, intense, and full of pressure. A lot of money is involved not only in the cost of creating an advertisement but also in the potential for revenue for the client. Some people describe advertising projects as hit-and-run operations. An ad is created, sometimes in a hurried atmosphere, but as soon as that assignment is completed, the creative team picks up another project and the hectic pace begins again.

Advertising professionals also change jobs frequently as a way of getting promoted. Companies like to hire people who have worked in other agencies. While this may seem a bit like recycling talent within the industry, it actually allows a flow of creative energy and ideas among agencies, keeping campaigns fresh.

The relatively rapid turnover in personnel creates many opportunities for those who wish to enter the field. A recent graduate in advertising design should have a portfolio full of advertisements and campaigns that show how they think and design. Creativity and being able to carry an idea through phases of the design process are vital skills in this fast-paced and competitive field.

Earnings

The average earnings for advertising designers are approximately $42,000. In many areas, salaries in this field overlap with those of graphic designers, mentioned above.

Advertising and Youth Culture

Our culture places a great emphasis on youth, and in the world of advertising, that generally means people in their twenties and thirties. This is the age group that advertisers find attractive, ambitious, and representative of the future. Young people are huge consumers of clothing, accessories, personal electronics, and beverages, and it is often young people we see pitching these products in ad campaigns. There is a reciprocal relationship between the models used in advertising and the products they are promoting. The attractiveness of the models affirms the value of the products, while desirability of the products reinforces our perceptions of the attractiveness of the models.

This doesn't mean that only young people are portrayed in advertisements. Ad agencies know a great deal about the target audience they want to reach for particular products. They must focus on the appropriate age group for each product. For instance, actors in their forties and fifties are more likely to appear in ads for Mercedes-Benz automobiles and for financial investment services, because they are perceived as more financially established and therefore more likely to purchase these products.

However, when you consider print and television advertising overall, you will see a higher percentage of young models for the majority of products.

Interior Design

Perhaps the first thing to understand about interior design is that it encompasses more than interior decorating. While it is true that interior designers are responsible for selecting fabrics, furniture, wall and floor covering, accessories, and lighting, that is only one part of their job. Interior design is also involved in preparing plans for the construction of a building's interior. At its root, interior design has as much to do with knowledge of architecture as it does with knowledge of the decorative arts.

Early in their educational training, designers learn a variety of skills that enable them to handle the technical as well as aesthetic aspects of the profession. Their studies include architectural drafting, two-dimensional drawn floor plans, reflected ceiling plans (the "floor plan" of the ceiling including lighting), elevations (front and side views of an interior space), paraline drawings (three-dimensional drawings using angles to project the walls vertically from a plan), and perspectives that are central to the interior design process.

Most interior design work is completed with the use of computers. Programming, furniture inventory, plans, elevations, and three-dimensional drawings may be produced quickly and with great accuracy using specially designed software packages. Students also study construction methods and materials, as well as information about basic mechanical, electrical, and plumbing building systems.

The aesthetic side of the profession includes knowledge of a full range of product lines (including fabrics, finishes, furniture, and accessories) that are used to add life to the interior space. Designers also learn about such issues as the history of design styles, color theory, and lighting.

Interior design work falls into two basic categories: residential and contract. Residential work involves designing for the home, including everything from apartments and lofts in the city to suburban residences and rural vacation homes. Residential design clients may be an individual, a couple, or an entire family, which means that the designer must be prepared to work with multiple opinions and needs.

The designer must think of the home as a social unit that centers around interrelated human needs and patterns of living, and issues ranging from the technical and aesthetic to those that are social and psychological must be addressed. The primary design issues, however, are related to aesthetics and the lifestyle of the home owner.

Most residential designers are self-employed or work in partnership with someone else. The residential designer is both a specialist and a jack-of-all-trades, because this work requires focused knowledge, skills, and a particular sensitivity to the needs of the client. For this reason, it constitutes a distinct and specialized segment of the design market.

Contract design is more varied and often more complicated because it relates to the health, safety, and welfare of the public. It includes interior design for grocery stores, department stores, restaurants, schools, hospitals, nursing homes, banks, theaters, shopping centers, and professional and business offices of all kinds. Contract design projects often include complex variables, and the aesthetic issues alone can be demanding. For example, the style preferences of the diverse kinds of people who pass through an interior space may have to be considered. Or it may be necessary to find a design approach that will be visually comfortable to a more limited and specialized range of people who use an interior space on a daily basis.

Health, safety, and welfare issues are a major consideration, as are issues of accessibility and ease of use for the disabled. Local building and fire codes must also be considered in contract work. The technical and design considerations for particular types of clients may be very exacting. For this reason, some clients may want a designer with experience in designing for their particular needs, which is often the case in the design of such specialized structures as hospitals or cruise ships.

Besides aesthetic and safety issues, there are a large number of technical considerations in contract design. These include such diverse elements as the client's electrical requirements for computers and other equipment, acoustical problems, lighting needs, budgetary matters, the psychological effects of color, and the social significance of office sizes and locations.

There are many different kinds of interior design projects, and the various requirements of each will depend on a number of factors. First, if the interior project is part of the architectural design for a whole building, the architects who design the building may have much to do with designing the interior skeleton of the structure. This is especially true if the building is being designed for the needs of a particular client, in which case interior designers may be more involved with color and the selection of fabrics, floor and wall coverings, furniture, and accessories.

Second, an architect may design a building for a developer that will be leased to tenants at various points after construction. In this case, the building will be designed with empty floor space, and an interior design team will be hired to create the structural configuration or shell of the interior space and to plan the aesthetic elements of the design project. The first part of the project will rely on design as well as technical skills and knowledge, and the second part of the design will focus on the decorative arts.

A Typical Contract Project

An interior design project involves a number of phases and develops over time. The process involves assessing the client's needs, developing a preliminary plan that shows how space for those needs will be organized, preparing drawings that present several aspects of the basic plan in more detail, presenting the plan to the client, coordinating with the client's contractor to establish the budget, and then making sure that the interior construction is completed according to the drawings. Let's consider a typical interior design project for an office building that may involve the following tasks (these do not necessarily evolve in a strict linear or time-sequence way).

Programming

The conceptual phase of the project begins by finding out what the client needs and proposing alternative design solutions. Determining what a client needs is called *programming*, a term that refers to the process of assessing a variety of needs and ways the interior space will be used. Programming will focus on the amount of total floor space required for the number of people working in or served by the client company, finding out what kind of space and technical requirements each person has, examining how various individuals interact with one another, and determining the organization's need for equipment, storage, offices, meeting space, and circulation (how people move through the interior). This is a very important stage in the life of the project, because the design team must accurately assess from the outset the client company's current as well as potential needs for space.

Schematic Design

The interior designer will next begin to develop ideas that are related to the client's program. The designer will sketch out general floor plans based on the client's various programming requirements, such as office space, work stations, furniture, and circulation routes.

As the project moves along, technical drawings, also known as drafts, will be used to indicate the precise measurements and locations for what needs to go into the existing space. If a new building is being constructed, some of this work will be designed by architects who specialize in designing interior space. The constraint on interior designers is that, in most states and provinces, they cannot create designs that modify existing structural elements used to support the building. Thus, any technical drawings by interior designers that are used to specify interior non-loadbearing construction will not include any work to be done on basic architectural elements in the building.

In addition to allocating and configuring the interior space, the designers must begin to think about basic aesthetic issues related to color, material, and finishes on walls and floors. Ideas about furniture and accessories also will be discussed during this stage. These issues must be developed with consideration for the kind of corporate image an organization is trying to promote. A company may want the interior to look very upscale and sophisticated, or it may want to convey a feeling that is more easygoing and comfortable. The type of institutional look that might work for a hospital would probably not be appropriate for a law firm. Each organization will have an image of itself that it wants represented by the atmosphere or character of its interior. So the interior designer must find a visual language that an organization can use to symbolically communicate a sense of itself to its employees and those that it serves.

Design Development

Once the designers have determined the client's program, prepared schematic drawings showing the interior space, considered the image the organization is trying to project, developed a few aesthetic approaches, and understood the client's budget constraints, the task is then to develop a specific design scheme.

At this point, the designer will move beyond general technical and aesthetic considerations to consider specific details. Precise floor plans will be laid out that show exactly where the furniture and accessories will be located. In addition, the specific kinds of product lines and colors for wall and floor finishes, ceiling, lighting, fabrics, furniture, and accessories for the interior will be selected. The designers will then make a presentation to the client, who will either agree to the design proposal, or more typically, will ask for refinements. Once a design has been approved and a budget is finalized, the project can move forward.

The next development phase involves making the design proposal a reality. Once the technical and aesthetic issues have been determined, a bid will be sent out to contractors who will do the various kinds of work required. A bid will also be sent out to dealers who carry the various product lines. Once the client has selected from among the bids, the orders for the various design products may be placed.

Construction Documents

The construction documents include technical drawings that show how the interior space is to be constructed and specifications that indicate exactly what kind of design products will be put into the interior. These documents legally bind all the parties involved. The drawings, for example, may indicate where a cabinet or workstation must be placed, and the specifications will indicate exactly what kind of cabinet and workstation are to be installed. The specifications also detail what furniture, lighting, and so forth are to be used in the project.

Construction Administration

The interior design team is responsible for quality control. In particular, they must be sure that the construction documents are followed exactly, which means making field inspections until the project has been completed.

Merging the Technical and the Aesthetic

Not all students who enter college to study interior design are aware that there are two sides to interior design work. As we have seen, interior design is an interesting blend of technical issues, such as those related to architectural drawings and knowledge of construction methods and material, and aesthetic issues—those related to color, fabrics, furniture, and lighting. It is important to have a clear understanding of the full range of requirements for the profession.

Size of Interior Design Firms

As with other kinds of design fields, the size of interior design firms may affect the range of work that a young designer will do. In larger firms, design tasks tend to be more specialized, although this is not the case in every large firm. In such companies, designers are asked to handle a variety of tasks so that more work may be done by fewer people, thereby reducing labor costs. In either case, however, a designer who is just starting out may spend most of the time drafting floor plans or elevations. It is also not likely that a young designer will have any contact with clients, unless a project is small.

Interior designers often work with architects. In fact, many of the larger architectural firms will have an in-house interior design department. In such cases architects and designers work together on a single project, especially when a firm is hired to design an entire building. On such a project, the architects design the interior and exterior skeleton, and interior designers are responsible for selecting the interior colors, fabrics, finishes, furniture, and accessories. In large renovation projects, the plans for interior construction may be drawn by architects or designers, depending on the nature of the work required.

Young designers have a better chance to get more varied work experience in smaller firms with fewer designers, where each member may have to pitch in and do a variety of tasks. A designer will still have to learn the ropes and spend time doing the less interesting though important work of drafting or computer aided design (CAD), but he or she may be able to move on to more varied tasks sooner than would be the case in a large firm.

Earnings

Interior design salaries vary widely with the specialty, type of employer, number of years of experience, and reputation of the individuals. Among salaried interior designers, those in large specialized design and architectural firms tend to earn higher and more stable salaries. Interior designers have median annual salaries of approximately $43,000. Earnings for those employed in architectural, engineering, and related services are $47,000; those working in specialized design services earn approximately $44,000.

For residential design projects, self-employed interior designers and those working in smaller firms usually earn a per-hour consulting fee, plus a percentage of the total cost of furniture, lighting, artwork, and other design elements. For commercial projects, they might charge a per-hour consulting fee, charge by the square footage, or charge a flat fee for the entire project. Also, designers who use specialty contractors usually earn a percentage of the contractor's earnings on the project in return for hiring the contractor. Self-employed designers must provide their own benefits.

Fashion Design

There is perhaps no other applied art field that is so deeply connected to the everyday lives of real people than fashion design. Fashion design is responsible for the clothing that we wear at home, school, and work. What we wear is just as relevant when we go to a baseball game as when we go to the ballet. Our clothing not only keeps us warm and protects us from the elements, it also helps shape who we are or want to be, both socially and psychologically.

Fashion design is one part of a larger network of industry relationships that also includes manufacturing and sales. Although fashion designers are primarily responsible for the actual design of clothing, they must also be mindful of whether standard manufacturing methods are suited to the materials and patterns of particular designs. They are also intimately concerned with the problems and prospects related to sales. In fact, design decisions are largely determined by a consideration of what will and will not sell.

Fashion design employs many people. Although there are some freelance designers, most professionals have staff positions in fashion design firms or companies that manufacture clothing. The garment industry in the United States and Canada is concentrated along the East and West coasts, but clothing is manufactured in many large cities, providing a variety of good career opportunities.

Design Process

The fashion design process begins with color. Color trends are set by the large mills that produce fiber, which is made into cloth and, ultimately, into clothing. The mills determine the characteristics of the fabric used to make clothing, and no characteristic is more important than color. Trends in color may vary over time, but basic seasonal trends are repeated each year: fall and winter typically feature dark, deep, and rich colors; spring includes chalk tones and pastels; and summer focuses on bright and vivid colors.

Based on the fabrics available for each season, fashion designers select a number of fabrics to work with. Once the fabrics have been selected, designers create the directional silhouettes (the shapes and proportions) for their line of clothing. Each "group" of garments a designer creates includes pieces that relate to each other. For example, a group of women's sportswear may include three tops, two jackets, one or two shirts, a pair of pants, a skirt, and a sports dress.

Any line of clothing will be organized around a design concept that includes such considerations as fabric and color, seasonal style, and specific design elements for the group. Initially, a number of design concepts may be considered, but a single concept will ultimately be selected. Once the design concept has been chosen, many quick sketches called *croquis* are developed to show what the specific design of each piece in the group might look like. Once these sketches are edited, the final design choices are made.

At this point, samples are developed to see what the garments will actually look like. The samples may undergo several adjustments and are refined at each step to perfect the fit. Finally, the finished garments are shown to buyers for large retail stores and specialty stores throughout the country.

Design Considerations

Fashion designers must address a variety of considerations related to their design ideas. Some of these are technical, but most focus on the needs, tastes, and buying patterns of various categories of consumers. Taking these human factors into account helps establish the marketability of clothing and, therefore, has everything to do with the design process.

Some technical considerations are related to manufacturing. For example, certain fabrics may be too delicate for particular kinds of construction methods. Other technical issues are related to the characteristics of fabrics and how they will be used. Designers need to know which fabrics will hold a crease, which will be comfortable in warm weather, and which will stand up to use in a washer and dryer. Each of these fabric characteristics is essential in selecting material for certain kinds of garments or garments designed for particular seasons.

Perhaps the most interesting design considerations are those based on a social and psychological understanding of people. These include gender, age, region of the country, season of the year, the intended uses of the clothing, and price points. The designer must consider all of these factors because they are important to the customer; in fact, they are designed into clothing as a basic part of marketing strategies.

The most basic design considerations are sex and gender. Almost all clothing is designed for the explicit difference in the way men and women dress, which is found in clothing for all age groups and almost all occasions.

It may seem that young men and women often appear to dress alike, particularly in casual clothes. While gender may not seem to be a significant factor for college-age consumers, that impression is not altogether correct. There are subtle yet important differences in the design of such items as jeans and sneakers for men and women. Physical differences between the sexes are also significant from a design point of view because of their differences in height, weight, and shape. So both the physical differences related to sex and the cultural differences related to gender need to be factored into fashion design.

Age is another basic factor that is related to design issues such as size, color, and style. Children grow rapidly from infancy through their late teens. Fashion designers must take age-related size differences into account, as well as changes in the shape of the human figure. Both men's and women's shapes change as they get older, and designers must keep this in mind when appealing to an older market. The figure is not the only thing to change, however. Designers also need to pay attention to taste and style preferences in clothing that are related to changes in lifestyle. Age-appropriate clothing becomes more important as people advance in years, because we want to wear clothing that reflects our current status.

Regions of the country and seasons of the year are also relevant design considerations. The kind of clothing as well as the choice of fabric, style, and color will vary depending on where in the United States or Canada the clothing will be worn. In states and provinces like New York, Ontario, Michigan, and Minnesota, clothing styles and fabrics need to be suited to cool or cold weather during much of the year. In the south and southwest United States, as well as in California, clothing needs to be light and is often colorful. Similarly, clothing needs will vary between summer and winter, especially in parts of the country that have significant temperature shifts between the seasons.

Designers need to be aware of these considerations but do not necessarily have to resolve the fashion issues related to each one whenever they begin a new design. That is because many designers will focus only on one established market area or category such as misses, teens, or active sportswear within a particular price range. In cases where the selection of a specialty area has resolved basic design issues, the designer will focus on matters related to color, style changes, and season.

The price point or cost of a garment is critically important from both a manufacturing and a marketing point of view. Customers expect the clothing of particular manufacturers to fall within a fairly narrow price range, and if price points vary too much, the clothing will not sell. This means that designers must select materials and styles that will keep the manufacturing costs where they need to be. It is also the case that the designers will offer a few different lines, each with a set price-point range, within their overall collection.

Cycle of Fashion Design

There are resource publications that help designers plan their colors and styles for the coming seasons. These publications come from companies that forecast or predict coming trends based on their analysis of changes that take place in style over time. The forecasts presented in periodicals such as *PromoStyl* and *Here and There* provide the fashion industry with ideas of what researchers believe will be in style during the next season. These forecasting publications give fashion designers a common frame of reference for long-range design planning.

Style and trends are important elements of fashion design. People generally buy new clothing before old clothing wears out because they want to keep up with changes in style. These changes are tied to a trickle-down trend in fashion development. Often, style changes begin with the most exclusive fashion designers like Karl Lagerfeld, Donna Karan, or John Galliano. As soon as their newest fashions come out, they are copied by other manufacturers who make less-expensive versions, sometimes with interpretations added. The knockoffs are sold either right away or during the next season for much less money. Other less-expensive knockoff versions of the garment may be sold perhaps two or even three seasons after the original design is shown. By the time a style trend has reached the lowest end of the market, it will have been abandoned by couture designers who have developed new fashion trends.

Earnings

Earnings in fashion design vary widely based on the employer and years of experience. Starting salaries tend to be very low until designers are established in the industry. Salaried fashion designers usually earn higher and more stable incomes than self-employed or freelance designers. However, a few of the most successful self-employed fashion designers may earn many times the salary of the highest paid salaried designers.

Median annual earnings for salaried fashion designers are about $63,000. Most earn between $43,000 and $88,000; while the lowest paid earn less than $30,000, and the highest more than $117,120.

A Final Thought

Working for a design company can be a very gratifying and rewarding career choice in the visual arts. Whether your interest lies in graphics, advertising, interiors, or fashion, you may build a lucrative and secure career in this area. The intricacies of the various design processes and the possibility of job mobility make this a very attractive field for many visual artists.

6

FREELANCE DESIGN

PROFESSIONAL WORK THAT is done without long-term or exclusive
commitments to one employer is known as *freelance* work. A freelance artist or designer actually runs an independent business that
sells services or products to a number of different clients, which
means that freelance professionals must have many talents and abilities. They must set up their own studio, order their own equipment and supplies, do their own public relations work, get their
own clients, set and maintain schedules, contract out work that they
may need to have done for a project, keep records, handle billing,
and take care of accounts receivable. They also need to actually do
the art or design work that they get paid to do.

One of the most distinctive characteristics of freelance work is
the need to balance a particular kind of independence with self-
reliance. We have seen that many fine artists function within this
type of balancing act, as do applied artists such as illustrators and
photographers. This means that freelance works best for those art-

ists who find that this kind of employment is sufficient to satisfy their social, psychological, and creative needs.

Illustration

Illustrators produce drawings and paintings that convey information or make an idea clear, work that is usually representational and sometimes has a very lifelike quality. Some illustration, however, relies much more on the artist's imagination to make a familiar image more interesting and eye-catching. An illustrator may also visually express an abstract idea or a human emotion. The needs of the client will dictate the specific nature of the illustration, but the final product will be similar to representational or figurative fine art. As you will recall from Chapter 3, this kind of art presents a stylized rendering of the real world. The image represents the thing being portrayed.

The object being portrayed and the image, however, are not the same thing. There is a very realistic painting by the French artist Rene Magritte that is entitled *The Treachery of Images*. Below a tobacco pipe, Magritte painted the phrase "Ceci n'est pas une pipe" ("This is not a pipe"), calling our attention to the fact that the painting is not a pipe, but rather an image of a pipe. Although this painting is an example from the world of fine art, it reminds us that illustrative renderings will always be an interpretation of the object being portrayed. In all cases, the artist adds a creative or distinctive touch to the image. Therefore, the fact that an illustration is made in response to a client's or art director's needs does not keep it from being art. It simply means that it is not the same as fine art.

Illustrations are uniquely suited as a means of representing certain kinds of images that cannot be shown through photography.

Perhaps the most obvious example would be images of people who were alive before photography was invented. If a client needs a picture of Shakespeare, for example, it would have to be an illustration. Or if an image is required for a place that it is not possible to photograph, such as the surface of a planet, a very deep part of the ocean floor, or an imaginary landscape, then an illustration will probably be called for. There are many such needs that only illustration can satisfy. Illustration may be created by use of a wide range of traditional media, but it is often produced in digital format, also.

Staff Positions

Although illustration is well-suited to freelance work, some illustrators hold staff positions in companies or work in firms that only handle illustration. A company that manufactures consumer products, for example, may have artists on staff who illustrate the products and the way they should be used. These drawings are usually technical in nature. Certain publications such as *Popular Mechanics* or the children's magazine called *Highlights* require a lot of illustration and may, therefore, have an illustrator on staff. Greeting card companies such as Hallmark Cards or American Greetings will have illustrators on staff. Beyond these rather limited situations, however, most work is done by freelance or independent illustrators.

Editorial Illustration

The work of illustrators falls into two basic categories: editorial and commercial. The differences between them are related to how much creative freedom the artist has. Editorial work is more interpretive and therefore requires more artistic individuality. This is perhaps why artists are more interested in doing this type of illustration assignment, even though the pay is less than it might be for commercial illustration.

Editorial illustrations are found in magazine articles, magazine and book covers, newspapers, and book texts. They attempt to portray something that has been written. The image may be rendered in a direct and literal way or, as is more frequently the case, in a creative and visually interesting way, depending on the nature of the text being illustrated and the publication in which the text appears. An illustrator doing a piece for a magazine article, for example, will read the article and then try to capture a central idea or theme in the illustration. An art director of a magazine who hires an illustrator may give the illustrator an idea of what kind of image is desired. Even in that case, however, the illustration will be very much related to the written text. An illustrator with a prominent reputation may have more freedom to interpret the ideas that need to be represented visually.

Commercial Illustration

Commercial illustration involves drawings or paintings that are used in corporate manuals, annual reports, brochures, textbooks, employee publications, direct-mail campaigns, television commercials, animation, advertising, and online applications. Such illustration is not used to accompany the kind of text that would be found in stories, articles, or on book covers. Therefore, the style requirements are different. This type of illustration is usually less interpretive and more realistic.

Another important area is artwork that is intended to be displayed at the "point of purchase" in retail stores. This involves an illustration that is used to catch the consumer's eye in a store or other marketplace. Such illustrations may help reinforce a television commercial, suggest a need for the product, or help link the product with a particular segment of the market. An example of point-of-purchase illustrations might be a tie-in between a movie and the Happy Meals sold at McDonald's—for instance, the *Pirates of the Caribbean* tie-in had illustrations of the characters from the film that represented toys found in the children's meals.

A Typical Assignment

What does a typical illustration job entail? Let's say that a regional Coca-Cola distributor wants an advertising agency to produce an eye-catching display ad that will be used to promote the sale of Coke at grocery stores. The art director, copywriter, and creative director from the agency meet to develop an idea for the ad, and then the art director makes a few comps (design sketches for the ad) and pitches the idea to the client. In this particular case, the art director wants the display ad to have an illustration that will be used to highlight the product. The idea involves using an illustration that shows cans of Coke bursting out of a tub of ice.

The art director already has examples of the work of a few illustrators on file. These illustrators will be asked to submit a bid on how much they will charge to produce the required illustration. Based on the bids and the samples, the client will then give the agency the go-ahead to hire the illustrator, who will take the comps, some photographs of the product, and any other visual material from the ad agency. In addition, the illustrator may want to find a tub or take a photo of a tub to use as a reference for the drawing.

A *tissue drawing* will be made that shows in outline form what the finished drawing will look like. The art director will either approve this or ask for changes; if changes are significant, the illustrator may charge more for the additional work. Once the drawing is approved, it will be transferred to the paper on which the final drawing is produced. This paper (or other material) is called a *board*. The next step involves making a very precise painting of what the art director requested: cans of Coke bursting from an ice-filled tub. Again, the art director will either accept the painting as it is or will ask for changes. Once it is finally accepted, the illustrator is no longer involved in the project, and the illustration becomes integrated into the display ad.

The same process is used to produce illustrations for print advertising in magazines and newspapers, which is a significant area of work for freelance illustrators. One reason the fees for such work are relatively high is that companies are willing to spend a lot of money to advertise their products. Advertising increases both sales and revenues for the company. Illustrators contribute to that income-producing system.

Stock Agencies

It used to be that new illustrations were commissioned for every project. Today there are companies that specialize in keeping a library of illustrations that can be sold through a catalog or CD. These companies are called *stock agencies*.

Many of these companies operate online. An Internet search for stock agencies will result in numerous leads, some for directories of thousands of companies that provide images in numerous areas.

Each agency will have a large number of such diverse illustration categories as famous people from the past, the insides of machines, or historical settings, to name just a few that clients may choose from. As we have seen, many of these images can only be produced through illustration. A growing trend in images is for illustrations that represent concepts rather than people, places, or things. A client may request an image that represents competitiveness, winning, hope, or human energy. Such conceptual categories give illustrators who produce work for stock agencies creative license to translate interesting ideas into concrete images.

Illustration for Children's Books

Most of us can remember a favorite book or two from childhood, and those fond memories will undoubtedly include the wonderful illustrations that were a part of the books. Whether it was Dr. Seuss, Richard Scarry, or Beatrix Potter, the illustrations probably made a lasting impression on you.

Children's books are wonderful from an illustrator's point of view because they require a high degree of creativity and imagination. The requirements for illustrations will of course vary depending on the age of the children for whom the book is written. Books for very young children will have many simple illustrations and relatively little text. For older children, the illustrations may be more complex and more inventive. In either case, illustrations for children focus on something that is immediately recognizable and something that is fundamentally human.

In most children's books, illustrations are used to help tell the story. They focus on parts of the story that are visually strong, include references to the main characters, or provide information about location. They may also add something to the story that is not actually present in the written text.

Sometimes an illustrator will collaborate with a writer and present a finished product to the publisher. Other times, a publisher will hire an artist to do the illustrations for a written story. An artist may even write the story and do the illustrations, which is often the most preferable option. In addition to issues of creative control and professional satisfaction that come from doing both parts of a book, there is a significant economic advantage. If a writer and illustrator work on the book together, they will split the royalties. An artist who both writes and illustrates a book will get full share of the royalties.

Getting a Start

Again, we find that there is a difference between the job market in major cities and in other parts of the country. For example, there are no illustration studios in New York, which means that all of the illustration work is done by freelance artists. This makes the market very competitive and yet at the same time very democratic. This is because the single most compelling factor in getting illustration work is the quality of one's artwork. As the prominent New York illustrator and fine artist Marshall Arisman has said, "It all comes down to the portfolio and what's in it." So a young illustrator just out of college with an excellent portfolio can get work. But, as Arisman emphasizes, there are many illustrators out there competing for assignments, which means that the quality of the work must be truly first-rate.

Although New York remains a major location for work, you don't necessarily have to live there to get the best illustration assignments from the top advertising agencies. It is also possible to send samples or slides of work to the art directors at magazines. The difficulty with that approach, however, is that magazines generally prefer a particular style that complements the content of the publication or that will be appreciated by its readers. Therefore, it is important to have a very good idea of the kind of illustrations that a magazine is likely to use before sending samples of your work.

Another route for getting work, particularly in smaller cities, is through an art representative. These are professionals who save illustrators the legwork of going to different ad agencies and showing their work. Art reps, however, are sometimes reluctant to take on illustrators who are just beginning. Unless an illustrator has a proven record of reliability and performance, the rep may not want to take a chance in making a recommendation to an ad agency. If the illustrator cannot produce work quickly enough or is difficult to work with, the judgment of the rep who promoted that person would be called into question by the art director at the ad agency. That is a situation that an art rep cannot afford. After all, the business of being a rep is also competitive, and they do not work for free. Reps get between 25 percent and 30 percent of the price of the illustration project as compensation for their efforts.

Computers

Since illustrations are sometimes created by the digital layering of existing images or text, they may be easily produced using computers. There are also a number of digital graphics programs that allow artists to produce drawings that look like work rendered through traditional media. The result is that drawing, as it is typically thought of, may not necessarily be central to an illustration.

Computers can simulate nearly all media, and the work created using drawing, pastel, or paint simulation is excellent. Most of the traditional image-making media and techniques may be done on a computer; it is even possible to simulate the look of watercolor. In fact, you often cannot easily tell when certain kinds of illustrations have been drawn with traditional media or with a computer.

However, it is important to remember that computers are simply tools. Despite their incredible technical potential, they do not create art any more than a pencil does. To be proficient using computers for illustration, graphic design, or anything else, it is imperative that artists be trained in basic art and design skills. This important subject will be discussed in more detail in Chapter 8.

Earnings

It is difficult to determine the earnings of self-employed illustrators, but those working for employers have median annual earnings of about $42,000. The middle 50 percent earned between $29,000 and $59,000, while the lowest ten percent earned less than $19,000, and the highest ten percent earned more than $80,000.

Photography

Photography is one of the most prevalent of the applied-art areas. Photographic images are everywhere—we see them in magazines, newspapers, newsletters, catalogs, brochures, book covers, websites, annual corporate reports, textbooks, restaurant menus, calendars, postcards, billboards, product packaging, store windows, and display advertising. Even baseball cards use photographs. While some photographic images are famous and seem to be a permanent part of our cultural heritage, most photographs are rather disposable. Once they are used for a particular commercial purpose, they disappear from our visual landscape.

There are also more cameras available now than ever before. The high quality of the technology and the low price of basic equipment make the medium accessible to a large number of people. The widespread use of digital cameras, image processing programs such as Photoshop, and the ease with which we can share photos have also increased the popularity of photography. There is still a world of difference, however, between an amateur with a camera and a professional photographer. That difference is a consequence of the consistently high quality of professional work, as well as the economic and occupational circumstances that characterize the field.

Staff Positions

There are not many staff positions for photographers. Newspapers and news services such as the Associated Press hire photographers, as do some specialty magazines such as *National Geographic*. But these jobs are scarce. In most cases, a magazine or any other business or individual who needs photographs will either hire an independent photographer or will buy photographs from a stock house.

Photographic Studios

Many independent photographers own their own studios, where they have a space set up with controlled lighting and other necessary equipment for in-studio shoots. Location photographers who travel on assignments may also have a studio. In this case, however, the studio may function more as a business office and base of operations than a place where photographs are taken. A studio may also include a darkroom for photographic processing, but in many cases, especially where color photography is involved, film will be processed and printed in laboratories that specialize in work done by professional photographers.

From a business point of view, a studio may be both an asset and a liability. The advantage is that a studio can give clients the sense of the photographer's permanence and stability, and it is a convenient place for conducting business and storing supplies and equipment. But a studio is also a monthly expense, and such bills as rent, utilities, and insurance must be paid regardless of how much time the photographer spends there.

Most photography studios are small—even the studios of internationally known photographers may employ as few as three or four people. The reason for this is that a single person can produce a photograph. By contrast, graphic design or advertising design may require the skills of a number of people. A photographer will need an assistant or two, plus someone who can take care of bookkeeping and scheduling. In some cases, a photographer may have an apprentice, known as a "second shooter," who can also do some of the more basic photography or work on small photographic assignments. Beyond that, not much more is needed. On those occasions where a large amount of equipment is required for a location shoot, freelance assistants may be hired for any number of days or weeks.

Thus, while independent photographers may have their own studios, they still function as freelance artists, especially from the point of view of art directors who hire them to shoot a particular assignment. These photographers work for themselves and do not have a permanent or exclusive employment relationship with a single company. Independent photographers may work on many assignments during the year. Although the assistants who work with them may be thought of as having staff jobs, these are not typically career positions. Instead, they are more similar to apprenticeship positions in that they provide good learning opportunities, but no one wants or expects to work at them for long. Freelance assistants are paid on a per diem basis and earn around $150 or more per day in smaller cities and more in larger cities. Most assistants aspire to own their own studios.

Like illustrators, many independent photographers have photo reps who show their work to ad agencies and design firms. They rely on photo reps because they are typically unable to devote enough of their own time and attention to important marketing and sales duties.

Specialization

Photography is highly specialized, with professionals photographing such diverse subjects as people, food, products, architecture, sports figures, automobiles, and fashion. Even these fields may be narrowed down to include those who specialize in photographing children, weddings, animals, or catalog ads.

Specialization has evolved out of the photographer's need to find work in a competitive market. It is a way of developing an expertise that art directors can turn to when they need to feel confident about the outcome of a photographer's work. Photographers may move from one specialization to another, but they generally stay within a familiar range.

Advertising photography includes what you find in magazines, newspapers, websites, and also in point-of-purchase displays. This type of work is done as part of a creative team that is coordinated by an art director at an advertising agency. The art director will typically specify what is required of the photograph. Experienced photographers who have been working with a particular agency or art director for a period of time may be able to make creative recommendations, but most often the photographer is hired to execute an idea that has come from someone else.

Although some photography fits the common perception of the field as being glamorous, many of the more lucrative assignments have little or no glamour. Catalog work is a case in point. Consider a company that sells industrial or commercial supplies and uses catalogs to show its products. These might involve such products as industrial lighting, heavy earth-moving equipment, small power tools, residential carpeting, or toilet seats. The products themselves may not be very glamorous, but they all need to be photographed. An ongoing relationship with a company that requires a lot of catalog photography can be an excellent bread-and-butter account for a photographer.

Stock Agencies

Stock agencies dealing in photographic images work similarly to those that handle illustrations. A stock agency will sell its photographs to anyone who needs a particular type of image. These photographs are usually generic images of mountains, sunsets, street scenes, dairy farms, fans at a ballpark, or people at the beach, for example. Other categories include travel, food, medical, underwater, geography, or industry. Each broad area is further broken down into subcategories. Industry, for example, may include such areas as computer production, steel manufacturing, and fiber optics.

These images are used in magazines, advertisements, and textbooks. A sociology textbook, for example, may require photographs of extended families (mother, father, children, and relatives) from several different cultures. Stock companies may have hundreds of photographs in that category from which editors may choose.

Stock photographs are often used when it is not practical to hire a photographer for a specific assignment. When there is an unexpectedly tight deadline, for example, a stock photograph may be obtained in a day or less. Or when it is too expensive to hire a photographer to fly from Chicago to shoot a street scene in Paris, a stock agency will have a large number of Parisian street scenes from which a client may choose.

Photographs are sold on consignment, with the photographer and the agency each getting 50 percent of the price. The sale price of a photograph depends on how it is to be used. For example, if it will be published in a small in-house newsletter, the lowest price for the image would be around $300. On the other hand, the cost of a photograph that will be used for an American Express marketing brochure that will be mailed to two million people may be as high as $10,000 or more.

It is not easy to get a start in stock photography largely because of the time and expense involved in developing a sufficiently large portfolio. A stock agency may require a photographer to submit a minimum of five thousand photographs—an enormous number that represents a very large investment of time and money.

Getting a Start

Most professionals in this field start out working as a photographer's assistant, but getting that first job can be tough. The key is persistence and the willingness to work hard. The industry abounds with stories of individuals who were willing to repeatedly ask for work with a particular photographer. In time, the photographer became sufficiently impressed by the display of commitment and determination to give the person a chance. Such persistence is good preparation for the kind of drive necessary to make it in the competitive world of professional photography.

A strong recommendation from a faculty member at an art college can help in getting a start as an assistant. An internship in which a student works with a photographer as part of his or her college education may also serve as a valuable entrance into a professional work situation.

The duties of a photographer's assistant involve a variety of menial chores, including scheduling photographic sessions, setting up studio shots, hiring models, loading film, and some lab work, such as film processing and ordering supplies. Assistants who work for location photographers will also do a lot of hauling and setting up of equipment at various locations. After working for a while, an assistant may be given small assignments that the photographer does not want to handle. These provide excellent experience and may pave the way for other assignments.

In addition to being hired as permanent assistants, many young photographers work as freelance assistants when photographers need their help for a particular job. Although this work lacks permanence and stability, it provides great opportunities to learn. Freelance assistants are exposed to a wide variety of photographic assignments, locations, professional equipment, aesthetic approaches and techniques, professional work habits, professional settings, and business skills. They are often hired to help with location assignments that sometimes require travel to foreign countries. The assignments will last anywhere from a few days to a few weeks, after which an assistant will hire on with another photographer.

Some photographers get their start by working in a photographic laboratory that processes and prints color as well as black-and-white film. Such labs are set up to handle work that comes in from professional photographers who ordinarily do not print their own color work. These professional labs have high standards and hire individuals who are well trained and technically competent. The salary range for beginning lab technicians is $20,000 to $25,000.

The quality of a young photographer's portfolio is often not as important as a willingness to help and work hard. This is especially true for those who start their careers by working as assistants. Other important attributes include reliability, self-motivation, and a cooperative attitude. The quality of the portfolio becomes more significant later, when a photographer begins to get work on his or her own. At that point, art directors and clients will want to look at samples of photography.

Some beginning photographers find work by looking for less competitive freelance assignments. For example, small magazines that are often local or regional in scope and that cater to a select readership make use of images to accompany text in much the same way that larger national publications do. In addition, small public relations firms need photographs of their clients or aspects of their clients' organizations. Companies like these, as well as larger advertising agencies and publications of all kinds, sometimes have a drop-off policy that allows photographers to leave their work to be reviewed and picked up at a later time.

Setting Up a Studio

Setting up a studio and working as an independent photographer takes a large initial investment. The major costs include all of the equipment necessary for either studio or location work. In addition to several kinds of cameras and many kinds of lenses, a photographer will need lighting equipment, tripods, and light meters. It is also important to have enough money available to pay rent and other bills for the studio space for at least six months before a sufficient amount of work comes in. The total setup cost for a studio may be anywhere from $200,000 and up depending on the city in which the studio is located. There are very few young professionals who have the financial resources to be on their own right out of college.

Computers

Taking a photograph is only one part of a process that leads to the finished product. There are many darkroom techniques used during the printing of a photograph that add to its final look. Most of these are done by a computer, and they play a significant role in professional photography.

Once a photograph has been taken and printed, the image may be scanned into a computer, where the digital information is manipulated and the photo changed in a variety of interesting ways. This is the process of photo retouching that used to be done by hand in the darkroom. Many of the photographs that you see in magazines have been manipulated in this way. Computers can add a sandy-looking quality, or they can add an antique look, which gives a photograph a somewhat soft and golden appearance. They can also make images look as though they have been subjected to a swirling process that gives them a dreamlike look. Once the desired effect has been created, you have a digital file and computer printout of a real photograph.

Earnings

The median annual earnings of salaried photographers is about $27,000. Most earn between $19,000 and $40,000, but the lowest paid earn less than $16,000 and the highest more than $57,000.

Salaried photographers, more of whom work full-time, generally earn more than those who are self-employed. Because most freelance and portrait photographers purchase their own equipment, they incur considerable expense acquiring and maintaining cameras and accessories. Unlike news and commercial photographers, few fine arts photographers are successful enough to support themselves solely through their art.

A Final Thought

In this chapter you've read about the work of illustrators and photographers, two specialized areas of the visual arts. You may see that, while some staff positions are available, the majority of these professionals work independently. If either of these career paths appeals to you, be sure that you have the temperament and commitment needed to successfully run a business. In addition to your artistic talent, you must be able to attract clients, pay the bills, and perhaps hire an assistant.

7

Careers in Art Education and Art Therapy

Teaching art and art therapy are closely related professional fields that have much in common. Their value lies in the benefit that people derive from the creative and expressive process of making art, which has considerable emotional and therapeutic potential. These fields offer excellent career opportunities for those who are committed to art and who like to work with people.

Teaching art involves the ability to bring out the special gift of visual creativity in those who already possess it. This can be an enormously satisfying experience—one whose value is widely recognized. Art teachers are respected for what they contribute to their students as well as to the community as a whole, and this respect may translate into relatively high salaries.

Most art teaching is done in two settings: public schools and the postsecondary level. The first involves teaching art in kindergarten through senior year in high school (K–12); the second involves teaching art in colleges and universities where the focus is more on professional training objectives. On occasion, there may be some occupational movement between the two settings as individuals move from one sector into the other. But for the most part, teachers who specialize in one area remain there throughout their careers. This is true in large part because of the different professional training requirements in each educational setting.

Art therapy also provides especially attractive career opportunities for individuals who enjoy art and derive satisfaction from helping others. In fact, the very essence of this field lies in helping others by involving them in art. The art therapist works in a variety of institutional settings as part of a therapeutic team that addresses clients' physical, emotional, and psychiatric needs. Those who work in this field must be knowledgeable about the expressive and communicative functions of art, as well as theories of human psychology and behavior and the practical aspects of art making.

Art Education

The term *art education* usually refers to a very specific occupational area that involves teaching art within the public school system. The two fundamental subdivisions in art education are based on the distinction between elementary (grammar school) and secondary (high school) education. Since art education in this setting is supported by public funds, its agenda is to educate all children in art, not simply those who present special talent.

The resources for and commitments to art education are somewhat mixed. On the one hand, all states and provinces certify teaching specialists in art on the elementary and secondary school levels. Virtually all schools or school systems have a visual arts program, which means that employment prospects are strong for art teachers who have just graduated from college. On the other hand, new teachers may not always find the teaching resources for art to be as plentiful as they might hope. In many cases, such things as a specialized classroom for teaching art, a written art curriculum, a full stock of art supplies and equipment, as well as adequate funding for art programs may not always be counted on.

Nonetheless, there is good reason to be optimistic about the prospects for art education. Professional organizations such as the National Art Education Association, with members throughout North America, work to promote values, ideas, research, leadership, advocacy, curriculum development, and professional development services necessary for the continued growth of the field. These efforts point to a general social awareness of and commitment to the role of art in elementary and secondary education.

Understanding the fundamental rationale for art education helps to explain the positive contribution it makes to the individual and society; it also explains what lies at the heart of the profession for art educators. The objectives of art education say something basic about what motivates individuals to pursue this career path and what the practice of the profession entails.

General Educational Philosophy

In the United States and Canada, art education is part of a general educational philosophy that seeks to provide students with the learning experiences they need to be fully developed individuals and to appreciate the world in which they live. A variety of educational goals have been articulated for public education under this banner. These include such broadly based objectives as fostering the growth and enrichment of the individual and establishing cultural links between the individual and other members of the community. Art education is consistent with both of these objectives.

Enriching the Individual

The future of children is influenced by their earliest learning experiences. This is true of the specific knowledge and skills they acquire as well as the basic capacities they develop. These capacities grow in value, much like economic investments. Art education expands a child's capacity for thought. It stimulates the imagination, brings to life a variety of concrete problem-solving experiences, and activates the potential for personal creativity. Early experiences with art also increase a child's capacity to translate direct personal experience into positive artistic expressions. This promotes a child's self-esteem and sense of productive accomplishment.

Another benefit of art education is its role in teaching young people to perceive the beauty that surrounds them. We sometimes take for granted our ability to appreciate the visual world, not realizing that the ability to perceive is a learned capacity and must be consciously developed. For example, you may have read that the Inuits living in Alaska do not have a generic word for snow but instead have a particular word or phrase for each kind of snow that they encounter, such as windblown, dry snow or light, fluffy snow with fat flakes. They are able to perceive different kinds of snow because they have learned to identify things of importance in their environment. In a similar way, children must learn a visual language that will enable them to perceive beauty in their world. The beauty they see lies in their capacity for perception.

It is possible to teach children about art without requiring them to actually make it, but that approach does not provide as much educational impact as one that links values, ideas, and experience.

As the old adage tells us: "What I hear, I hear; what I see, I remember; what I do, I understand." As we will see shortly, current approaches to art education integrate a range of art-related ideas with the art-making process.

Community-Based Goals

Art education makes an impact not only on the developmental potential of individuals but also on their ability to live with one another in a social context. Developing a language and appreciation for art helps establish the foundation for a shared culture. This is especially true for those people who desire to understand their ties to specific cultural communities, but it also applies to our need for integrative links between those diverse communities.

The integrative and community-making potential of art education exists, in part, because of art's symbolic nature. Images convey meanings that either bring people together or pull them apart. Art education can help create community ties because it paves the way for an understanding of symbolic communication. The increased public visibility of fine art and applied art images makes this an increasingly important role for art and art education. Thus, a primary goal of art education in relationship to the community is to develop literacy in the arts. The growing public role of art means that more and more people will be exposed to it and will need to be able to evaluate its various meanings.

Teaching Art

The general educational objectives related to the individual and the community may be achieved by teaching children specific knowledge, skills, and information about art. To do that, children are taught how to make art and, in so doing, how to understand it and appreciate it. Art education gives students the opportunity to explore the specific content of various art disciplines, such as drawing, painting, printmaking, and photography. By making art, students not only develop a greater understanding of what art is, but they also prepare themselves for the possibility of more advanced art making.

This means that there must be specific curriculum-based art programs. One approach to art curriculum that was developed by the Getty Center for Education in the Arts is a discipline-based art education program (DBAE), which is based on the simple idea that art has content and can be taught. The DBAE curriculum emphasizes four areas: making art, art history, aesthetics, and art criticism. With this type of curriculum, the ideas the students learn about art are fused with the physical skills of making art. This or any other kind of art curriculum needs to be taught in a sequential and developmental way, because children should not be introduced to educational material that they are not ready to handle.

A well-developed art education curriculum for students at any age level in the public school system should be rich in content and should provide the teacher with a useful guide for classroom instruction. Such a program allows the teacher to focus on visual elements of art, such as space, light, color, line, form or shape, and texture. These elements should be part of a teaching strategy that includes making art in the classroom to learn the meaning of various aspects of art; classroom discussion of each element based on examples from other cultures or historical periods; and homework assignments involving independent art projects. The specific content of the art curriculum always needs to be tailored to the developmental levels of the various age groups.

A successful art teacher needs more than a conceptual understanding of art. Teachers must also be artists, which means that they must be educational specialists who understand the basic methods, materials, and concepts of their particular disciplines. Not only do art teachers need to be artists and to understand art, they also need to have a variety of other knowledge and skills. In particular, they need to have good language skills and must be able to communicate well with children.

Getting a Start

Undergraduate programs require that art education majors do student teaching in a public school system. The teaching experience typically takes place in a high school during a college student's senior year. A student who does well as a student teacher may be given first preference when a job becomes available in that school system. This arrangement is also advantageous to the school, which is able to hire someone who has already demonstrated an ability to work successfully as an art teacher. Teachers are also recommended for positions through professional networks that exist among school systems and various art education programs in art colleges and universities.

There was a time when art teachers were paid less than in other subjects, but fortunately this is no longer the case. Median annual earnings of kindergarten, elementary, middle, and secondary school teachers ranged from $43,580 to $48,690 in 2006. According to the American Federation of Teachers, beginning teachers with a bachelor's degree earned an average of $31,753 in the 2004–05 school year. The estimated average salary of all public elementary and secondary school teachers in the 2004–05 school year was $47,602. Salaries vary depending on experience and the geographic location.

Teaching Art in College

Art programs in higher education play essentially two roles. First, they are often included as part of the general education requirements that all students in a particular college or university must take. These requirements give students the opportunity to take college-level studio art courses that enrich the individual and provide an opportunity for a hands-on experience in cultural production. These courses are very limited in scope; for the most part, they provide an introductory-level curriculum. Second, art programs provide a major area of academic concentration for students who wish to study art in depth. There are a variety of such programs that will be covered in Chapter 8.

Postsecondary art teachers may work on either a full-time or part-time basis. Each has a particular role to play in the educational life of the college or university. They also have a particular meaning in the professional lives of artists who teach. Together, full-time and part-time faculty constitute the backbone of the teaching profession in higher education.

Part-Time Teaching

Part-time or adjunct teachers play a vital role in higher education. Many adjunct faculty members choose to teach part-time because they work full-time in their professional careers and want to share their experience with others. This is especially true for faculty who teach a professional area in which they have expertise as practitioners. This is one of the characteristics of professional education in general. The faculty teach subjects that are directly related to their professional practices—this is true for artists in all of the fine art and applied art areas.

This can be an advantageous situation for some artists, especially for those who are at an early phase of their professional lives or who have successful careers as fine artists or freelance artists. The time they devote to getting their careers started or to lucrative professional work may prevent them from teaching more than one or two courses at a time. Part-time teaching enables these artists to supplement their income, share their knowledge with students, and derive whatever prestige may be gained from working as a college teacher. Thus, for some artists, teaching on a part-time basis permits them to combine the best of both academic and professional life.

Part-time faculty often enhance students' learning experiences because they generally bring the most current and interesting professional issues into the classroom, allowing students to stay abreast of the latest artistic trends, technical developments, and professional concerns. This is particularly important in the applied arts, where changes in the practice of the profession directly impact what students need to learn. Part-time teachers of fine art are not only able to add fresh insight to the creative process, but they also serve as positive role models who provide practical advice about a wide range of professional issues.

Adjunct teaching is not without its drawbacks, however. Adjunct faculty may make $5,000 or more for each course they teach, but they usually do not receive additional benefits, such as health insurance and retirement programs. In addition, some full-time faculty members in an art college or university may view adjunct faculty as outsiders whose involvement in the education of students should be limited. But despite these difficulties, part-time faculty make a positive contribution and will continue to play a significant role in higher education for many years.

Full-Time Teaching

Full-time college teaching is an especially attractive career option for artists. The pay for full-time faculty is good, though not enough to make a person wealthy, and the hours, benefits, and working conditions are highly desirable. An especially attractive aspect of college teaching is that artists and designers may continue to pursue professional work for which they earn additional income. In fact, they are encouraged to do so. In this way, not only do art teachers add many thousands of dollars to their annual income, they also enhance their academic careers by continuing their professional work. Being professionally active will help art faculty to earn promotions and salary increases and to receive the guaranteed job security of tenure.

Art faculty spend only a few hours each week in the classroom. Depending on the particular institution, they may teach anywhere from twelve to eighteen hours per week. There are, however, additional obligations. They are required to meet with students, evaluate student work, serve on committees, attend meetings, and participate in other college activities. Even with all of these responsibilities, however, full-time art faculty spend far less time working at their primary jobs than individuals in other professional fields.

Faculty members are also eligible to go on sabbatical once every six or seven years. A sabbatical will usually last either a half year at full pay, or a full year at half pay. The idea is that faculty need time to get away from teaching to pursue their own professional interests, which may then be brought back into the classroom to enrich the content and process of teaching.

Academic and professional achievement is rewarded through a system of promotions that includes the ranks of lecturer, assistant professor, associate professor, and full professor. Criteria for promotion differ among schools but will typically include specified years of teaching experience, professional development such as gallery exhibits, and service to the school. Each promotion carries increased prestige and usually a salary increase as well. Earnings for college faculty vary according to rank and type of institution, geographic area, and field; and faculty in four-year institutions generally earn higher salaries than those in two-year schools. According to a 2006–2007 survey by the American Association of University Professors, salaries for full-time faculty averaged $73,207. By rank, the average was $98,974 for professors, $69,911 for associate professors, $58,662 for assistant professors, $48,289 for lecturers, and $42,609 for instructors.

Many faculty members have significant earnings in addition to their base salary from consulting, teaching additional courses, research, writing for publication, or other employment. In addition to sabbaticals, many college and university faculty enjoy unique benefits, including access to campus facilities, tuition waivers for dependents, and housing and travel allowances. Part-time faculty and instructors usually have fewer benefits than full-time faculty.

Art Therapy

Art therapists do not make art themselves as part of the practice of their profession, but they provide a therapeutic service by enabling others to make art. Nonetheless, they must be trained as artists, with a background that includes a thorough and practical understanding of how people experience the creative process. This understanding is essential in helping others utilize art creation as a medium for self-exploration.

As a profession, art therapy offers interesting choices in relationship to other career options in art. Although practitioners must grapple with issues that lie at the heart of art making, such as the personal significance of creativity and the expressive nature of art, they must pursue their own creative impulses on their own time. This will not be a satisfying situation for everyone, particularly for those who believe that the core of their professional lives must revolve around actually making art. On the other hand, art therapy offers occupational stability and a clearly defined set of employment possibilities, as well as a good salary and benefits.

A Human Service Profession

Art therapy is part of a larger complex of interrelated professions that are dedicated to helping people who have different kinds of problems. Therapeutic teams work in settings that include substance abuse clinics, alcoholism treatment programs, veterans administration hospitals, general hospitals, shelters for battered women, child-life support programs in hospitals, community centers for the elderly, nursing homes, prisons, schools, and psychiatric hospitals. The broad range of clients, patients, and inmates served by these institutions suggests how versatile the healing potential of art therapy can be.

Determining which particular professions should be represented on a therapeutic team will depend on the institutional context in which clients or patients are served. Psychiatric hospitals, nursing homes, and prisons have different populations, each of which has specific needs that may be best addressed by appropriate human service professionals. Depending on the institutional setting, art therapists may work with doctors, nurses, psychiatrists, psychiatric nurses, mental health workers, psychologists, psychiatric social workers, physical therapists, and corrections officers. In addition, each of these may specialize in the particular problems of the clients they serve. Thus, a psychiatric social worker, along with an art therapist, may have expertise in drug-related problems, geriatric problems, or problems related to children in general hospitals who are receiving treatment for serious medical conditions.

An important aspect of art therapy is that it serves a number of interrelated goals. The quality of the art produced by patients, however, is not necessarily one of them. The real value of art therapy is that it may be used to diagnose emotional problems or as part of a treatment plan to resolve those problems, and it may be used to assess the patient's progress during treatment.

Therapeutic Rationale

The assumption that lies behind art therapy is that the creative art-making process serves diagnostic and therapeutic goals. At the center of both of these goals is an extremely important idea related to the groundbreaking theories of the psychiatrist Sigmund Freud. He believed that some experiences and resulting emotions are so unpleasant that our conscious mind will be unable to acknowledge them. Thus, prior experiences may be so difficult to deal with on the conscious level that we are unaware of their effect on us. These experiences become repressed and are pushed into what Freud called the subconscious mind.

Diagnosis

Art therapy tries to address the difficulties that people experience because of their repressed thoughts and feelings. The creative experience is believed to be so spontaneous and to come from such a deep-seated source in our consciousness that it allows repressed feelings and experiences to reach a level of conscious awareness. As a result, art therapy plays an important role in diagnosing emotional problems because it enables the underlying source of problems to be revealed through art.

Imagine, for example, a young child who is troubled by problems in her family. When asked about why she is unhappy, she may not be able to identify the source of her feelings. But when asked to draw a picture of her family, she may unintentionally leave one of her parents out of the drawing. This may provide a diagnostic clue that the difficulty lies with that parent. The drawing that springs from a deep and spontaneous source in her mind may allow her repressed feelings to be unintentionally revealed through the images she has produced.

This does not mean that any picture with a family member missing is necessarily an indication of a problem. Nor does it imply that all art should be analyzed for hidden meanings. The point is rather to show the kind of thinking that lies behind art therapy. Art therapy enables patients to express themselves freely and, therefore, is useful as part of the diagnostic phase of the therapeutic process. Once the repressed emotion is revealed, it can become the focus of therapeutic intervention.

Art therapy is useful as an expressive outlet for adults in the same way. Some adults, especially those who are fairly well educated and articulate, are able to use their language ability as a way to maintain a certain type of emotional distance from other people. They may be very good at discussing professional issues or world politics on an intellectual level, but they may not be as open or as insightful about their own emotional lives. Intelligence by itself does not bring repressed thoughts and feelings into full consciousness. Again, art therapy is a helpful means for revealing the unconscious mind.

Treatment

Diagnosis is only one part of art therapy. Art therapy can also be used as part of a therapeutic treatment plan for patients. The art-making process not only allows patients to gain insight into repressed thoughts and feelings, it also provides them with positive experiences that have therapeutic value. These positive experiences are a valuable part of a patient's treatment and recovery.

Exactly what those positive experiences might be and what their value is to the patient depends on several factors. These include the patient's specific problem, the kind of therapeutic approaches that are thought to be helpful, and the particular way in which making art contributes to the recommended treatment plan. In general terms, the creative experience leads to therapeutic results because it helps develop a patient's self-esteem, encourages a patient's sense of reality through figurative image making, and provides a record of the patient's therapeutic progress as it is revealed through the art they make. The issue of self-esteem is especially important. In a culture that sometimes seems to place too much emphasis on the surface characteristics of people, art therapy helps give the person a solid core of positive experience.

Treatment is also facilitated when patients see the visual evidence of their own previously unrecognized problems. Patients sometimes resist the interpretations that others make of their thoughts and feelings. But those interpretations are supported when patients actually see visible indications of what other people are able to detect.

Other treatment objectives are related to the use of art therapy in groups within various types of institutional settings. These group experiences involve artistic assignments that patients work on together or by themselves. Group activities make a larger demand on patients' interpersonal skills, encouraging them to communicate ideas, share materials and work space, respect the rights of others, and accept the institutional rules related to social behavior. If they are unable to do so, therapy provides a focal point for resolving difficulties related to relationships with other people.

These may seem like very simple and ordinary aspects of group interaction, but they may be fraught with tension for people who have serious emotional, physical, or behavioral problems. These social skills may also be especially difficult when they involve the highly personal and private act of making art in a social setting. The special value of art therapy is that it provides patients with an opportunity to resolve the problems related to bridging the gap between intense self-preoccupation and the needs of others.

Assessment

A patient's artwork provides information about how she or he is responding to treatment. For example, a patient may claim to be feeling better but continue to draw pictures of violence, death, or other themes that have been associated with an underlying emotional or behavioral problem. This means that art therapy is a valuable assessment tool that reveals significant differences between what patients say and what they are actually thinking or feeling.

Therapeutic Alliance

One of the satisfying aspects of the profession is the close bond that develops between the art therapist and the patient. In fact, their relationship must be based on a high level of mutual trust and respect. A significant potential source of trust stems from the fact that the therapist is also an artist. The therapist's belief in art therapy derives from the therapist having actually experienced the therapeutic effects of art making.

The shared experience of making art forms an important basis for the trusting communication that helps the patient and therapist discuss the possible symbolic significance of the images that are produced. This means that language skills also play a significant role in the work of art therapists, who use their skills to help patients sift through the veil of emotional entanglements and discover the value of their own creativity.

Therapeutic Team

As mentioned earlier, the art therapist works as part of a therapeutic team. In an institutional setting, several human service professionals are responsible for the treatment and rehabilitation of patients. Each team member adds some specialized expertise to the patient's care; and doctors, psychiatrists, psychologists, nurses, and art therapists must work together to provide the best possible opportunities for therapeutic diagnosis and intervention.

In order to accomplish this, they work together to develop a treatment plan that provides a therapeutic approach designed to address the particular recovery needs of a patient. Typically, members of a therapeutic team will meet two or three times each week to discuss a patient's progress, reporting on their efforts to help the patient and on the ways in which the patient has responded to those efforts. Treatment plans are adjusted as necessary, based on these meetings. Thus, each member of the therapeutic team serves as a valuable part of the coordinated effort to provide patient care.

Professional Associations

Both the American Art Therapy Association (AATA) and the Canadian Art Therapy Association (CATA) have played major roles in shaping the professional and educational requirements of the field.

They have been active in defining standards for professional practice and ethical conduct as well as guidelines for education and research. A master's degree is the established entry-level requirement for the profession. You will find additional information about the profession, as well as lists of art therapy programs that are approved by both societies, at their respective websites. Visit www.arttherapy.org for information about programs in the United States. Canadian information is available at www.catainfo.ca.

A Final Thought

The careers in this chapter offer a unique opportunity for those who wish to combine their artistic talents with helping others. If you would like to teach art, you should decide which age group best suits you and focus your educational training on fulfilling the necessary requirements. If you plan to work in art therapy, you should also think about which client base best suits you and direct your training toward working with that population.

8

EDUCATION OF ARTISTS

MOST OF US have our first real experience with art in grammar school, where art projects are often part of the normal classroom curriculum. At the high school level, separate classes in art are also available, since most school systems with a sufficient budget make some provision for art instruction. These early encounters with art are important because they expose young people to the creative process and introduce them to the pleasures of making art. Moreover, developing the ability to produce satisfying art enables students to view themselves in new and positive ways. This also forms the basis for further training in art.

Family members also provide early experiences with art by stimulating and encouraging creative activity in children. Many artists come from families with some background in creativity. While it is not altogether clear whether those creative impulses are genetic or learned, these influences enable people to develop the visual sensitivity and the eye-hand coordination that is necessary for making art.

Private Art Instruction

Almost every community has one or more organizations that offer art classes for young people and adults. Art instruction is sponsored by church groups, community centers, civic organizations, and the YMCA. In addition, private classes may be offered in people's homes. Individualized private instruction has the advantage of providing students with more personal attention than they might receive in other settings. These classes make art fun, and they often begin the lifelong process of making art.

There are also a variety of art centers that specialize in different levels of instruction. Some include a broad curriculum of art and craft courses that are recreational in nature. Most have basic and intermediate drawing classes, which can be a useful way to learn the fundamental drawing skills needed as preparation for more advanced art training at the college level. Art centers offer a wide range of courses for everyone—children, teens, and adults. In addition to basic drawing and painting, courses may cover such diverse subjects as photography, calligraphy, cartooning, comic book art, jewelry design, papermaking, wood carving, origami (Japanese paper folding), ceramics, silk painting, weaving, and interior decorating.

There are also residential art centers that are designed for more advanced students who are already involved with art as a career. These advanced training centers offer courses in drawing, painting, and sculpture by well-known artists. Such courses are typically taught as part of an on-campus program that includes accommodations and meals. These programs allow students to pursue intensive individualized studio work under the tutelage of distinguished professionals.

Credit and Noncredit College Courses

Art instruction is also available through the community education division of art colleges and universities, where you will find evening and weekend classes in drawing, painting, sculpture, and photography, as well as illustration, graphic design, advertising design, and interior design. These classes are usually taught by experienced artists and designers, and they provide a serious introduction to the various fields. If you want to get the feel of what rigorous art training is like, these classes offer an opportunity. Some colleges have more advanced levels of training for those who are already working in a professional art or design field.

This type of course may or may not be a credit class. Classes for credit meet for a certain number of hours during a semester and may be counted as college courses if you decide to apply as a full-time student at an art college or university. Noncredit classes usually meet for a fewer number of hours and cannot be transferred into a college degree program.

Online Art Instruction

Although most online distance learning is based on written text, there are companies that provide online image-based instruction for art and design as well. Instruction ranges from the basics of drawing to sophisticated website design. Instructors assign projects that students complete using a graphics software program, and they send their work to the instructor as an attached e-mail file. The instructor then reviews the work and sends comments and suggestions back to the student. Students in online courses also chat with one another and share ideas, insights, and experiences.

Art College and University Programs

Art colleges and universities offer a fairly specific range of programs, most of which include drawing, painting, sculpture, printmaking, photography, architecture, computer art, film, video, industrial design, illustration, glass, ceramics, and fiber. In addition, there are more specialized programs, including toy design, textile design, cartooning, yacht design, landscape architecture, and book art.

While these suggest the range of programs available, they do not exhaust the specialized areas of study within the programs. These programs are usually taught by faculty with expertise in a particular field. Their expertise will give students access to unique educational opportunities. There are also interdisciplinary options that allow students to formulate specialized curricula that are tailored to their own interests.

A number of private art colleges and hundreds of universities and liberal arts schools offer various types of art programs. It is important to remember that there are significant educational differences between art colleges and art programs in other institutional settings. There are also significant differences between the basic kinds of degree programs they offer. The first and most important distinction is that between a bachelor of arts (B.A.) degree in art, and a bachelor of fine arts (B.F.A.) degree.

The B.A. degree is not typically regarded as professional preparation for an art career because of the limited number of studio art courses it requires students to take. Such programs usually provide fewer technical and conceptual training courses than a B.F.A. degree. Students who receive a B.A. in art take approximately one-third of their courses in art, providing students with hands-on experience and a channel for individualized creative growth. Such programs provide a good introduction to art and serve as a solid foundation for graduate-level training.

The B.F.A. degree is regarded as the undergraduate professional degree in art. Programs that offer the B.F.A. usually require as many as seventy-two to seventy-eight credit hours or more. This translates into as many as twenty-five studio art courses, which is considerably larger than the number of courses typically required in B.A. degree programs in art. While a number of artists go on to get a master of fine arts (M.F.A.) degree for advanced art training, the B.F.A. is sometimes the only degree both fine and applied artists receive. Today, however, the M.F.A. degree is becoming more and more common for professional artists and designers.

Another important consideration in choosing a degree program is whether it is offered in an independent art college or in a liberal arts college or university. An art program in a liberal arts college or university will be one among many different programs, including business, engineering, nursing, and liberal arts. The independent art college, by contrast, will have art as its primary educational focus.

There are advantages to both settings. On the one hand, an art program that is part of a larger institution may be better for students who want a more conventional educational experience and who find curricular diversity and involvement in campus life appealing. On the other hand, those who want a more specialized educational setting where energies and resources are devoted primarily to art may feel more at home in an independent art college.

Some art schools, like the Atlanta College of Art, Otis College of Art and Design, and the Minneapolis College of Art and Design, for example, use the term *college* in the name of the institution. Some schools, however, do not. In fact, there are many excellent art colleges granting the B.F.A. that do not make an explicit reference to their degree-granting status in the title of their institution. Examples of such institutions would be the School of Visual Arts (New York), School of the Art Institute of Chicago, Rhode Island School of Design, or the Kansas City Art Institute. Some of these schools grant the M.F.A. as well. Visit a school's website or read its catalog carefully to determine its degree-granting status and to find information about academic programs. Information about these schools may also be obtained from the Association of Independent Colleges of Art and Design.

Choosing an Art School

You will face many options when you are looking for an art school, but you needn't feel daunted by the task. The key to selecting the right institution is getting as much information as you can. High school guidance counselors and art teachers have information about art schools, and they provide a good starting point as you begin to research which school is right for you. You will also find information about art schools and programs at www.petersons.com, where you can also research application procedures and financial aid resources.

Make a list of the schools that interest you based on the preliminary information you obtain from your research. You can find a great deal of information about a school's basic educational mission, its academic programs, the degrees offered, as well as the background of faculty members and profiles of graduates. Information is also provided about tuition, fees, and admission procedures.

Another excellent source of information is National Portfolio Day. This is actually a series of events during which a large number of art school representatives gather in one place to meet with students, review their portfolios, and answer questions. There are about twenty-five to thirty portfolio day events each year that are open to students in the United States and Canada. For complete information on National Portfolio Day, visit www.portfolioday.net.

The institutions that participate in National Portfolio Day are all members of the National Association of Schools of Art and Design (NASAD), which accredits art and design programs in colleges and universities and helps to ensure a high level of academic quality among participating institutions. Information about NASAD and the schools that it accredits is available at www.nasad .arts-accredit.org.

The National Association of College Admission Counselors sponsors the National College Fair, which also provides valuable information about art colleges and universities. There are about thirty-five of these fairs around the country. Visit www.nacac net.org for information.

Once you have narrowed your choice of schools down to a manageable number, you should plan a visit to each one of them. Although this seems like quite a task, it is a valuable way to get a feel for the spirit of the school and to see whether it can be your home for the duration of your studies.

It isn't necessary to have a clear idea about exactly which area of art you plan to study in college. Although some schools will encourage students to indicate a basic area of interest when they apply, many schools do not. They know that students who are applying to an art school may not yet have enough information to choose a major area of study. These schools often provide a foundation-level curriculum in the freshman year, which allows students exposure to various art disciplines, media, and art-making processes before they concentrate on one area. It is also not uncommon for students to change their majors more than once while they are in college.

Getting into an Art College

The three primary factors that contribute to getting into art school are your high school grades (in both art and academic courses), the Scholastic Aptitude Test (SAT) or the ACT score, and your portfolio of artwork. For students who are transferring from another college (whether an art school, a community college, a liberal arts college, or university), college grades are an additional factor. Students who apply from a foreign country other than Canada or another English-speaking country will also have to score adequately on a standardized language test, such as the Test of English as a Foreign Language (TOEFL).

The significance of your grades, test scores, and portfolio varies if there is a noticeable difference between them. For instance, a student with an average portfolio and excellent grades may have a better chance of being accepted than a student with an average portfolio and weak grades. Similarly, a student with a strong portfolio and good grades will have a better chance than one who has a strong portfolio and weak grades.

The portfolio is the one part of the admission process that separates art students from those who are seeking admission to other programs. Your portfolio should include the art or design work that you want the admissions committee to consider as examples of your work. Most schools want to see twelve to fifteen pieces of work, and regardless of the area in which you plan to major, perhaps the single most important works to include in the portfolio are life drawings. If your interest is photography, you should consult admissions personnel to ask about portfolio requirements.

If you plan to apply to an art college, you should take at least one basic drawing course and then draw from life as much as possible. Drawings that are copies of other drawings or photographs are of less value. Other artwork may be required by the particular college admissions requirements and may include photographs or drafting, depending on the type of program to which you are applying.

Scholarships and Loans

Although art education can be expensive, there are many grants, loans, scholarships, work-study programs, and payment plans to help defray the cost. Grants are an especially good source of funds because the money is typically based on a student's financial need and does not have to be paid back. The federal government has established Pell Grants, which provide money directly to individual students. There are also Supplemental Educational Opportunity Grants that are available for students who demonstrate exceptional financial need. In addition, states provide a variety of grants that may be used in addition to the federal grants.

Campus-based funding sources involve federal money that is funneled to students through colleges and universities. The Perkins Loan Program, for example, provides money to schools, which in turn loan money directly to their students. The Supplemental Educational Opportunity Grant is another federal funding source that is available to colleges and universities that is passed on to students.

Many students take out loans for college through banks, credit unions, or savings and loan institutions. The Stanford Student Loan is one of the most frequently used programs. The Supplemental Loan for Students provides additional loan money for students who are deemed financially independent of their parents. In addition, parents of college students may take out educational loans for their children through the Parent Loans for Undergraduate Students (PLUS) program.

Scholarships provide direct aid to students and come from a wide range of sources. The National Merit Scholarship is a major source of money that comes from the National Merit Scholarship Corporation. Scholarships are also provided by a variety of state government programs and local civic groups, as well as private and religious organizations. Like grants, scholarships do not have to be repaid, but they are typically awarded to students with a record of high academic achievement. Most colleges and universities also make scholarship money available to their own students.

Beyond these sources, colleges have a variety of financial plans for students, including installment payments, prepayment plans, and work-study options. Colleges and universities understand the burden of paying for an education and have many ways to help ease the load. Consult the financial aid office at the college you plan to attend for complete information about available financial aid. High school counselors can also help students to prepare their financial aid applications.

B.F.A. Degree Programs

A bachelor of fine arts degree, like other undergraduate programs, takes four years of full-time study to complete. The first year usually includes a foundation curriculum, which is required of all students in a particular school and might typically include a drawing course, a design course of some kind, a course on color, perhaps an elective studio course, and a writing and literature course. Depending on your major, you may find a greater range of foundation programs in some schools, which may include more specialized studio courses and liberal arts courses. By the time you begin your second year, you will usually have selected a major in one of the art or design areas. Some schools also allow students to pursue an individualized curriculum that is usually interdisciplinary in nature and integrates the subject matter of more than one art or design discipline.

Selecting a major will enable you to specialize in such studio areas as drawing, painting, sculpture, printmaking, photography, illustration, graphic design, or advertising design. The curriculum within each department addresses a full range of technical, aesthetic, and professional issues. Courses are taken in a loosely structured sequence that is intended to increase your exposure to what you need to learn. By the time you begin your final year, you will work much more independently and will be expected to produce work that is at or near a basic professional level.

The heart of a degree program is the studio art courses, but there is another area in the curriculum that should be emphasized as well. This involves the general range of liberal arts courses that students in all B.F.A. programs are required to take. About one-third of the course work will be in such areas as literature, history, philosophy, psychology, sociology, economics, mathematics, and science, and you will be expected to be able to read and write with a degree of proficiency that will allow you to fulfill your need for professional-level communications.

The particular curriculum at art colleges and universities will vary not only in terms of the art areas taught but also in terms of the structure of each program. For example, not all schools offer interior design or art education. In addition, at some schools the four basic fine arts areas may be a part of what is called the fine arts major, while at other schools each area constitutes a separate major. In either case, the content of particular areas of study is fairly similar among schools.

Drawing

The term *drawing* is widely used and may refer to everything from technical drafting to loose sketching. When it is used to describe a particular approach to making fine art, the term becomes even more ambiguous. That is because a variety of media may be used to create an art product that takes on a number of different looks. Some drawings look like what you might think of as a pencil or ink drawing, but those that are produced with crayons, charcoal, computers, paint, or some combination of these media may not. In fact, a college drawing program is likely to include a course that explores the basic question, "What is a drawing?" You will find that there are many answers.

To get to those answers, however, you will start with the basics. Most schools continue to emphasize figure drawing as the foundation not only of drawing as a discipline but also of other art areas as well. Beyond learning the basic techniques of line and shading used for rendering, you will develop a more individual approach to expression through drawing. Courses evolve in a progressive fashion from fundamentals to more advanced problems to personal aesthetic goals.

Drawing is not offered as a major or area of concentration in all art schools. One reason is because drawing is sometimes regarded as a means to an end rather than an end in itself. Thus, it may be used to sketch out ideas on paper for paintings, sculpture, or printmaking. Another reason is that drawing is used as the basic medium for illustration, which is often emphasized in the curriculum rather than the process used to achieve it.

When there is a focus on drawing as an end in itself, the results bring the artist and the viewer in touch with the oldest and most direct of the various art media. Drawing predates writing as a form of personal expression and communication. It is also perhaps the most portable of all media—artists sketch endlessly wherever they go. There is an immediacy and authenticity about it that many artists enjoy. Once a mark is set on paper, it is a permanent record of an artist's impulse or intention. For that reason, drawing has an honesty and purity about it that has been the foundation of all art making for centuries.

Painting

There was a time when it was easy to identify painting. Paintings were made with oil paint or some other paint medium that was applied to the two-dimensional surface of a rectangular canvas. Many paintings are, of course, still made that way. But today, work that is classified as painting is not at all limited by those constraints. Painting is done with anything that will stick to a surface that may or may not be two-dimensional. In fact, the boundaries of painting and sculpture are sometimes blurred because the application of surface color is becoming more accepted in sculpture and because painting has sought a variety of three-dimensional surfaces.

You will learn how to manipulate paint as a physical medium, using such paints as oil, acrylic, egg tempera, and encaustic (melted wax mixed with pigment). You will also learn how to build stretchers (the frame on which canvas is hung), to stretch and fix canvas on frames, and to prepare the canvas with gesso or other substances so that paint will properly adhere to its surface.

Learning how to paint involves developing the use of technique as a means to solving personally formulated aesthetic problems. At the basic level, you will develop your skills through the study of color, space, shape, form, texture, and surface. In addition, most art schools begin with a focus on traditional subjects, such as the figure, still life, and landscapes. At the more advanced level, you will work independently and will be encouraged to explore your own ideas.

Sculpture

As with other areas of fine art, sculpture has a long tradition of materials and methods but is currently undergoing significant changes. An undergraduate program in sculpture will provide you with the opportunity to become familiar with those traditions and to take your work into new areas. Sometimes the venue in which work is installed becomes part of the artwork itself. In such cases, a room or an exterior space is transformed into an installation exhibit.

Perhaps the one consistent characteristic of sculpture is that it requires the ability to address three-dimensional spatial problems. You will learn not to think only in spatial terms; you will also learn the methods and materials required to create three-dimensional forms. Such concepts as shape, form, symmetry, and surface will be explored through the techniques and materials of sculpture. You'll learn to use such traditional materials as clay, stone, wood, metal, paper, resin, and fiberglass. But less conventional materials are now becoming common as well, including tools, household and industrial products, mounds of soil, wire, used tires, street signs, electronic equipment, shopping carts, trash cans, fish tanks, food cans, glass, plastic, hay, mud, used clothing, and anything else you might imagine.

Printmaking

Printmaking involves course work that focuses heavily on the technologies of the discipline. These technologies include relief, intaglio, lithography, and screen printing. As with other art-making disciplines, each printmaking methodology is characterized by distinctive kinds of appearances. Printmaking is deeply rooted in the long history of fine-art image making, yet it has become a standard medium for even the most avant-garde aesthetic approaches.

A major part of a printmaker's education involves learning the four basic technologies. Relief printmaking works in the same way that rubber stamps produce images. The process begins by making cuts into the surface of wood or linoleum and then applying ink to the raised surface. Paper is then pressed onto the inked surface and an image appears.

Intaglio is made in the reverse way. Shallow scratches or marks are made on the surface of a copper or steel plate. Ink is rubbed into the marks and then the rest of the ink is wiped off the surface area that has not been scratched or marked. Paper is then pressed onto the metal plate with sufficient force so that it picks up the ink that is held within the marks that have been made in the surface of the plate.

Lithography is a somewhat involved process of printing from a flat stone or metal surface on which the image to be printed is ink-receptive and the blank area is ink-repellent. The ink-receptive areas form the image-making surface of the stone or metal surface. Screen printing basically involves a process of stenciling that is done through a fine mesh of fabric.

Photography

Photography programs usually begin with an introduction to the technology of image making. Learning the technology of photography involves familiarity with different kinds of cameras, filters, lenses, film, and lighting equipment, as well as various darkroom procedures and techniques. Through these procedures you will learn that a great deal of the photographic image happens after the picture is taken. Beyond basic film developing, darkroom techniques include hand mixing and applied emulsions, color separation, solarization, bleaching, toning, and hand coloring. Courses in electronic imaging will introduce you to still video cameras, scanners, and the software for image processing.

In addition, most schools emphasize the differences between studio and location shooting. Within these differences, programs focus on such specializations as still life, portraiture, architecture and interiors, landscapes, illustration, fashion, travel, news, and photojournalism. Beyond the various issues of technique and application is the concern with learning photography as a means of personal expression. This is just as important in the various applied photography uses as it is in fine art photography.

Interior Design

The technical requirements of interior design are demanding and numerous. As a result, undergraduate programs are often highly structured to ensure that students will be exposed to all of the course material they need. In addition to a wide variety of technical skills and information, students must become familiar with the design principles, styles, and product lines they will use to create safe, comfortable, and appealing interiors.

Because interior design focuses on structural and aesthetic issues related to spaces inside a building, you will learn to create floor plans, elevations, axonometric perspectives, and reflected ceiling plans to convey design ideas as well as technical information to clients, contractors, and vendors. Initially you may learn to draft by hand, but you will quickly learn to use and rely on computer-aided design (CAD) programs. In addition, you must become familiar with various kinds of building and mechanical systems, including heating, ventilation, and air conditioning. Building and fire codes are typically taken into consideration, especially for interiors that serve the public. Courses that focus on such specialty areas as acoustics and lighting are also valuable for interior design students.

You will learn to focus on the client's needs and to build a design concept around those needs. A design concept will define an aesthetic approach for a client. In addition to structural issues established by the design concept, consideration will also be given to color, fabrics, floor covering, furniture, and accessories.

All of these various elements are integrated into a curriculum that focuses on the process of interior design, and you will learn how to utilize these elements to satisfy the needs of particular types of clients. Interior design programs will typically offer courses that focus on issues and problems related to a variety of interiors, such as those required for families, professional offices, large corporations, retail stores, theaters, restaurants, schools, and other kinds of institutions.

Advertising Design and Graphic Design

Advertising design is concerned with teaching students technical skills, creative thinking, and problem-solving abilities. The technical skills include all of those methods and materials that are used to actually make the advertisements. Your studies will include the use of computers to make two- and three-dimensional designs that may include still images as well as motion graphics. The final product may also integrate text, typography, illustration, photography, and video.

The other basic educational goal is creative thinking. Here you will be taught how to solve the client's basic problem—selling a product. Courses will emphasize such issues as how to establish advertising themes, advertising strategies that develop over time, ethical issues, legal questions, social conditions, and demographics. Language skills are emphasized so that you learn how to make verbal presentations to clients.

The educational goals for graphic design are similar to those in advertising design; the primary difference is in the nature and objectives of the final design. Graphic design is used to instruct, inform, or call attention to institutions, products, and ideas. Your studies will teach you the technical and conceptual skills necessary to produce package design, brochures, logos, websites, and environmental design systems that fulfill those goals. While a broad range of skills should be developed, you will most likely be encouraged to focus on a particular area of interest in preparation for the development of your portfolios.

Illustration

This is a professional discipline that is closely tied to advertising design and graphic design. Illustration is often a component of the work done in these fields and is seldom used outside of some kind of design context. These three areas are closely connected on the academic level and are, therefore, often part of a single department in art colleges or university art programs.

There are also obvious and significant differences between these areas. As we saw in Chapter 6, illustration is often similar in general appearance to representational fine art drawing or painting. While studying illustration, you will be expected to learn basic technical skills using various media including pen and ink, pastel, paint, and computers. An emphasis will be placed on teaching you how to use these skills as a means of conveying ideas visually. In addition, you'll be encouraged to develop a personal style that will set you apart as an illustrator.

M.F.A. Degree Programs

If you decide to pursue a master of fine arts degree, you'll be expected to refine your technical skills and develop a personal body of advanced-level work. On the undergraduate level, you receive a solid introduction to the techniques and skills of a number of different disciplines. At the graduate level, your focus will be on the skills and techniques of one particular discipline. That focus will typically include mastering conventional materials and methods of the discipline, but it will also include a deep exploration of experimental approaches to making art.

Some students shift focus from one area of undergraduate study to a different area in a graduate program. Someone who majored in painting as an undergraduate, for example, may enter a graduate program to study illustration. This is important because it provides an additional level of educational flexibility as you discover your real professional interests. If you do make such a change, however, you should be prepared to refocus on learning new technical skills.

Becoming technically proficient will serve to develop your personal vision as a graduate student. This vision involves the approach that you will take in expressing ideas. The individual style that is typically associated with a mature artist is a manifestation of the concepts that lie at the heart of artistic creativity, so style and conceptual content work in an interdependent relationship to convey the full and multifaceted intention of art.

The content of art is important at the graduate level, and students often spend a large amount of time engaged in research to strengthen it. Although research may include experimentation with the tools and methods of art making, it may also mean developing a body of knowledge and ideas that support conceptual content. This type of research involves becoming intimately familiar with art history, as well as with a broad range of liberal arts areas.

A Final Thought

You now have a basic understanding of the career options in the visual arts, as well as a more detailed knowledge of what will be expected of you as an art student. Perhaps the information in this book has helped you to focus your interest toward a specific area of the visual arts or has provided useful information about the personal characteristics and educational background you will need to pursue a visual arts career. Whatever the case, may you find satisfaction and rich reward as you strive to achieve your goals.

APPENDIX

Professional Organizations

Advertising Club of New York
235 Park Ave. S, 6th Flr.
New York, NY 10003
theadvertisingclub.org

American Art Therapy Association, Inc.
5999 Stevenson Ave.
Alexandria, VA 22304
arttherapy.org

American Association of Museums
1575 Eye St. NW, Ste. 400
Washington, DC 20005
aam-us.org

American Association of University Professors
1012 Fourteenth St. NW, Ste. 500
Washington, DC 20005
aaup.org

American Craft Council
72 Spring St., 6th Flr.
New York, NY 10012
craftcouncil.org

American Federation of Arts
305 E. 47th St., 10th Flr.
New York, NY 10017
afaweb.org

American Institute of Graphic Arts
164 Fifth Ave.
New York, NY 10010
aiga.org

American Society of Interior Designers
608 Massachusetts Ave. NE
Washington, DC 20002
asid.org

The Art Directors Club
106 W. 29th St.
New York, NY 10001
adacglobal.org

Association of Artist Run Galleries
591 Broadway, Ste. 2A
New York, NY 10012
gallerydriver.com

Association of Hispanic Arts
P.O. Box 1169
New York, NY 10029
latinoarts.org

Association of University Interior Designers
auid.org

Canadian Architectural Certification Board
710-1 Nicholas St.
Ottawa, ON K1N 7B7
cacb.ca

Canadian Art Therapy Association
catainfo.ca

Canadian Association of University Teachers
2705 Queensview Dr.
Ottawa ON K2B 8K2
caut.ca

Canadian Crafts Federation
457 Queen St.
P.O. Box 6000
Fredericton, NB E3B 5H
canadiancraftsfederation.ca

Canada Council for the Arts
350 Alberta St.
P.O. Box 1047
Ottawa, ON K1P 5V8
canadacouncil.ca

Canadian Museums Association
280 Metcalfe St., Ste. 400
Ottawa, ON K2P 1R7
museums.ca

Color Association of the U.S.
315 W. 39th St., Studio 507
New York, NY 10018
colorassociation.com

Design Management Institute
101 Tremont St., Ste. 300
Boston, MA 02108
dmi.org

Federation of Canadian Artists
1241 Cartwright St.
Vancouver, BC V6H 4B7
artists.ca

Graphic Artists Guild
32 Broadway, Ste. 1114
New York, NY 10004
gag.org

Interior Designers of Canada
717 Church St.
Toronto, ON M42 2M5
interiordesigncanada.org

International Center of Photography
1114 Avenue of the Americas
New York, NY 10036
icp.org

National Architectural Accrediting Board
1735 New York Ave., NW
Washington, DC 20006
naab.org

National Art Education Association
1916 Association Dr.
Reston, VA 20191
naea-reston.org

National Association of Artists' Organizations
308 Prince St.
St. Paul, MN 55101
naao.net

National Cartoonists Society
341 N. Maitland Ave., Ste. 130
Maitland, FL 32751
reuben.org

Professional Photographers of America
229 Peachtree St. NE, Ste. 2200
Atlanta, GA 30303
ppa.com

Professional Photographers of Canada
ppoc.ca

Society of American Graphic Artists
32 Union Station, Rm. 1214
New York, NY 10003
clt.astate.edu/Elind/sagamain

Society of Graphic Designers of Canada
Arts Court, 2 Daly Ave.
Ottawa, ON K1N 6E2
gdc.net

Society of Illustrators
128 E. 63rd St.
New York, NY 10021
societyillustrators.org

Recommended Reading

Books

The following books address various aspects of fine and applied art careers in greater detail. There are a great many books available that can be useful resources in planning your career; those listed here are offered as a starting point for your research.

Alliance of Artists' Communities. *Artists' Communities: A Directory of Residencies that Offer Time and Space for Creativity*, 3rd ed. New York: Allworth Press, 2005.

Arango, Maria. *Art Festival Guide: The Artist's Guide to Selling in Art Festivals*. Lulu.com, 2007.

Audette, Anna H. *100 Creative Drawing Ideas*. Boston: Shambhala Publications, 2005.

Bamberger, Alan. *The Art of Buying Art*, 2nd ed. Phoenix: Gordon's Art Reference, 2007.

Burke, Sandra. *Fashion Artist*, 2nd ed. Burkepublishing.com, 2006.

Cox, Mary, and Michael Schweer, eds. *Artists & Graphic Designers Market 2007*. Cincinnati: Writers Digest Books, 2007.

Crawford, Tad, and Susan Mellon. *The Artist-Gallery Partnership*, 3rd ed. New York: Allworth Press, 2008.

Cullen, Kristen. *Layout Workbook: A Real-World Guide to Building Pages in Graphic Design*. Gloucester, Mass.: Rockport Publishers, 2007.

Darley, Suzanne, and Wende Heath. *The Expressive Arts Activity Book: A Resource for Professionals*. London: Jessica Kingsley Publishers, 2007.

Davis, Ron. *Art Dealer's Field Guide: How to Profit in Art, Buying and Selling Valuable Paintings*. Jacksonville, Fla.: Capital Letter Press, 2005.

Fariello, M. Anna, and Paula Owen, eds. *Objects and Meaning: New Perspectives on Art and Craft*. Lanham, Md.: Scarecrow Press, 2005.

Goldberg, Jan. *Careers for Color Connoisseurs & Other Visual Types*, 2nd ed. New York: McGraw-Hill, 2005.

Gordon, Barbara. *Opportunities in Commercial Art and Graphic Design Careers*. New York: McGraw-Hill, 2003.

Grant, Daniel. *Selling Art Without Galleries: Toward Making a Living from Your Art*. New York: Allworth Press, 2006.

Graphic Artists Guild. *Graphic Artists Guild Handbook: Pricing & Ethical Guidelines*, 12th ed. New York: Graphic Artists Guild, 2007.

Greenhalgh, Paul. *The Persistence of Craft: The Applied Arts Today*. London: A&C Black, 2002.

Heller, Steven, and Marshall Arisman. *Inside the Business of Illustration*. New York: Allworth Press, 2004.

Hobbs, Jack A., and Jean C. Rush. *Teaching Children Art*. Long Grove, Ill.: Waveland Press, 2006.

Hume, Helen D. *The Art Teacher's Book of Lists*. San Francisco: Jossey-Bass, 2005.

Jennings, Simon. *The New Artist's Manual: The Complete Guide to Painting and Drawing Materials and Techniques*. San Francisco: Chronicle Books, 2005.

Kelby, Scott. *The Digital Photography Book*, volume 2. Berkeley, Calif.: Peachpit Press, 2008.

Kelby, Scott. *The Digital Photography Book*, volume 1. Berkeley, Calif.: Peachpit Press, 2006.

Koster, Joan B. *Growing Artists: Teaching Art to Young Children*, 3rd ed. Florence, Ky.: CENGAGE Delmar Learning, 2004.

Landa, Robin. *Advertising by Design: Creating Visual Communications with Graphic Impact*. New York: Wiley, 2004.

Lang, Cay. *Taking the Leap: Building a Career as a Visual Artist*, 2nd ed. San Francisco: Chronicle Books, 2006.

Liberatori, Ellen. *Guide to Getting Arts Grants*. New York: Allworth Press, 2006.

London, Barbara, et al. *Photography*, 9th ed. Upper Saddle River, N.J.: Prentice Hall, 2007.

Malchiodi, Cathy. *Art Therapy Sourcebook*, 2nd ed. New York: McGraw-Hill, 2006.

Mauro, Lucia. *Careers for Fashion Plates & Other Trendsetters*, 3rd ed. New York: McGraw-Hill, 2008.

McAndrew, Clare. *The Art Economy: An Investor's Guide to the Art Market*. Dublin: Liffey Press, 2008.

McKelvey, Kathryn. *Fashion Source Book*, 2nd ed. London: Blackwell Publishing, 2006.

McNulty, Tom. *Art Market Research: A Guide to Methods and Sources*. Jefferson, N.C.: McFarland & Co., 2006.

Mills, John. *Encyclopedia of Sculpture Techniques*. London: Batsford, 2005.

Mitton, Maureen. *Interior Design Visual Presentation: A Guide to Graphics, Models & Presentation Techniques*, 3rd ed. New York: Wiley, 2007.

Morioka, Noreen, and Terry Stone. *Color Design Workbook: A Real-World Guide to Using Color in Graphic Design*. Gloucester, Mass.: Rockport Publishers, 2006.

Pedersen, B. Martin. *Advertising Annual 2007*. New York: Graphis Press, 2007.

Poehner, Donna, and Erika O'Connell, eds. *2007 Photographer's Market*. Cincinnati: Writers Digest Books, 2007.

Risatti, Howard, and Kenneth R. Trapp. *A Theory of Craft: Function and Aesthetic Expression*. Chapel Hill: University of North Carolina Press, 2007.

Rubinstein, Raphael, ed. *Critical Mess: Art Critics on the State of their Practice*. Lenox, Mass.: Hard Press Editions, 2006.

Samara, Timothy. *Design Elements: A Graphic Style Manual*. Gloucester, Mass.: Rockport Publishers, 2007.

Simmons, Linda L. *Interactive Art Therapy*. Binghamton, N.Y.: Haworth Press, 2006.

Smith, Constance, and Susan F. Greaves. *Internet 101 for Artists*, 2nd ed. Nevada City, Calif.: ArtNetwork, 2007.

Tangaz, Tomris. *Interior Design Course: Principles, Practices, and Techniques for the Aspiring Designer*. Happauge, N.Y.: Barrons Educational Books, 2006.

Udale, Jenny, and Richard Sorger. *The Fundamentals of Fashion Design*. Lausanne, Switzerland: AVA Publishing, 2006.

Villenueve, Pat, ed. *From Periphery to Center: Art Museum Education in the 21st Century*. Reston, Va.: National Art Education Association, 2008.

Vitali, Julius. *The Fine Artist's Guide to Marketing and Self-Promotion: Innovative Techniques to Build Your Career as an Artist,* 2nd ed. New York: Allworth Press, 2003.

Wheeler, Alina. *Designing Brand Identity: A Complete Guide to Creating, Building, and Maintaining Strong Brands,* 2nd ed. New York: Wiley, 2006.

White, Brian Marshall. *Breaking into the Art World: How to Start Making a Living as an Artist.* College Station, Tex.: Virtualbookworm.com Publishing, 2005.

Williams, Arthur. *The Sculpture Reference: Contemporary Techniques, Terms, Tools, Materials and Sculpture.* Springfield, Tenn.: Sculpture Books, 2004.

Zeegan, Lawrence. *Secrets of Digital Illustration: A Master Class in Commercial Image-Making.* Hove, UK: RotoVision, 2007.

Zeegan, Lawrence. *Fundamentals of Illustration.* Lausanne, Switzerland: AVA Publishing, 2006.

Periodicals

There are numerous periodicals devoted to many aspects of the visual arts. Following is a just a sampling of what is available; each title is followed by the name of the publisher. Some of the periodicals publish job opportunities and funding sources. Web addresses are provided for those publications that are also available online.

Applied Art Publications

Applied Arts Magazine
Applied Arts, Inc.
appliedartsmag.com

Ceramics Monthly
American Ceramics Society
ceramicsmonthly.org

Eye: International Review of Graphic Design
Haymarket Business Publication
eyemagazine.com

Graphic Design Journal
Society of Graphic Designers of Canada

Graphis Advertising Journal
Graphis Press Corp.

Idea: International Advertising Art
Japan Publications Trading Company

Inside Fashion
21st Century Media, Ltd.

Metalsmith
Society of North American Goldsmiths
snagmetalsmith.org

Pottery Making Illustrated
American Ceramics Society
potterymaking.org

Print
F&W Publications
printmag.com

Textile : Journal of Cloth and Culture
Berg Publishers, Ltd.

Fine Arts Publications

American Artist
Nielsen Company

American Illustration
Amilus, Inc.

American Photo
Hachette Magazines, Inc.
popphoto.com/americanphoto

Art Business Today
Fine Art Trade Guild

Art Education
National Arts Education Association

Art Therapy
American Art Therapy Association

Artist's Magazine
F&W Publications
artistsnetwork.com/artistsmagazine

Camera Arts
Shine Media Group
cameraarts.com

Fine Art Connoisseur
Streamline Media
fineartsconnoisseur.com

Fine Canadian Art
Heffel Fine Art Auction House

Illustration
Illustration
illustration-magazine.com

International Artist
Australian Artist
international-artist.com

Modern Painters
Fine Arts Journals Ltd.
modernpainters.co.uk

Object
Centre for Contemporary Craft

Photo Techniques
Preston Publications
phototechmag.com

Scholastic Art
Scholastic, Inc.

School Arts: The Art Education Magazine for K-12 Art Educators
Davis Publications, Inc.

Sculpture
International Sculpture Center
sculpture.org/redesign/mag

*Studies in Art Education: A Journal of Issues and Research in Art
     Education*
National Art Education Association

Women's Wear Daily
Fairchild Publications, Inc.
wwd.com

About the Author

Dr. Mark Salmon received his B.A. from the University of Hartford, and his Ph.D. in sociology from New York University. He served as chairperson of the Humanities and Sciences Department as well as the Interior Design Department at the School of Visual Arts in New York City and academic dean at the Atlanta College of Art. He is also the former New York State commissioner (downstate) of the National Association of Academic Affairs Administrators. Dr. Salmon serves as director of the National Conference on Liberal Arts and the Education of Artists, as editor of *Art & Academe: A Journal for the Humanities and Sciences in the Education of Artists*, and as codirector of the Institute for Visual Arts Research. He is the author of a number of articles on various aspects of the education of artists and designers. Dr. Salmon is currently vice president for academic affairs at Otis College of Art and Design.